SHARING IN THE SUCCESS OF THE DIGITAL ECONOMY

A Progressive Approach to Radical Innovation

**Edited by Robert D. Atkinson,
Michael McTernan and Alastair Reed**

policy network

ITIF | INFORMATION TECHNOLOGY
& INNOVATION FOUNDATION

ROWMAN &
LITTLEFIELD
——— INTERNATIONAL
London • New York

Published by Rowman & Littlefield International, Ltd.
Unit A, Whitacre, 26-34 Stannary Street, London, SE11 4AB
www.rowmaninternational.com

Rowman & Littlefield International, Ltd. is an affiliate of Rowman &
Littlefield
4501 Forbes Boulevard, Suite 200, Lanham, Maryland 20706, USA
With additional offices in Boulder, New York, Toronto (Canada), and
Plymouth (UK)
www.rowman.com

British Library Cataloguing in Publication Information Available
A catalogue record for this book is available from the British Library

ISBN: PB 978-1-78348-503-1

Library of Congress Cataloging-in-Publication Data

Sharing in the success of the digital economy : a progressive approach to radical innovation /
edited by Rob Atkinson, Michael McTernan and Alastair Reed.
pages cm
ISBN 978-1-78348-503-1 (pbk.) -- ISBN 978-1-78348-504-8 (electronic)
1. Electronic commerce--Europe. 2. Economic development--Technological innovations--Eu-
rope. 3. Employment forecasting--Europe. I. Atkinson, Robert D., editor.
HF5548.325.E85S53 2015
303.48'33--dc23
                                    2015006158

∞™ The paper used in this publication meets the minimum requirements
of American National Standard for Information Sciences Permanence of
Paper for Printed Library Materials, ANSI/NISO Z39.48-1992.

Printed in the United States of America

CONTENTS

III: A ROADMAP FOR EUROPEAN PRODUCTIVITY GROWTH

ABOUT THE CONTRIBUTORS

Robert D. Atkinson is the founder and president of the Information Technology and Innovation Foundation (ITIF), a Washington, DC-based policy thinktank.

Birgitte Andersen is director of the Big Innovation Centre, London, and runs a thought leadership forum on Intangible Gold.

Matt Brittin is the president of Google's business and operations in Europe, the Middle East and Africa.

Daniel Castro is director of the Center for Data Innovation, Washington, DC.

Julian David is chief executive of techUK, which represents the UK tech sector.

Paul Hofheinz is the director and co-founder of the Lisbon Council, a Brussels-based thinktank.

Michael McTernan is acting director of Policy Network, a London-based international thinktank and network.

Jonathan Murray is co-founding partner of Innovia Ventures, a New York-based technology consultancy.

Alastair Reed is a researcher at Policy Network, a London-based international thinktank and network.

Andrew Sharpe is founder and executive director of the Ottawa-based Centre for the Study of Living Standards (CSLS).

Nick Sohnemann is the founder and managing director of Future-Candy, an innovation consultancy, and head of the InnoLab at Hamburg Media School.

Kathleen Stokes is senior researcher on digital education and the collaborative economy for Nesta, a London-based innovation charity.

Desirée van Welsum is senior ICT policy consultant, The World Bank and associate partner at Innovia Ventures.

Matthew Whittaker is chief economist at The Resolution Foundation, a London-based thinktank focused on living standards.

THE PROGRESSIVE POWER OF CREATIVE DESTRUCTION

Robert D. Atkinson

A long time ago in a galaxy far, far way, progressives stood for progress. Indeed, in the US, progressivism represented the culmination of America's response to the creative disruption of the industrial revolution of the last half of the 1800s. In contrast to the populist opposition that preceded them, progressive reformers did not want to stop the movement to industrialisation and the great disruptions that stemmed from it; rather they wanted a government to humanise that new economy and ensure that its benefits spread to all.

Unfortunately with similarly rapid change from both globalisation and technological innovation roiling our world today, many progressives have reverted to a populism which seeks to reverse these fundamental forces. For many progressives now, economic change is "red in tooth and claw" leading more to destruction than creation, and pain, especially for workers swept up or swept aside by change; and it is better to seek stasis and stability through regulation, anti-corporate opposition and more generous income support policies. Emblematic are comments from the former French industry minister Arnaud Montebourg, now replaced by the more reformist figure of Emanuel Macron, who stated that when it comes to innovation that can destroy existing companies, "well, we have to go slowly."

But economists are largely in agreement: creative destruction stemming from technological innovation is a fundamentally positive force for it almost always leads to the replacement of less efficient, lower quality, and/or less innovative activities with more efficient, higher quality and/or more innovative activities. To be sure there are cases where innovations are welfare-detracting; in other words, innovations that while serving one particular group do not benefit the overall economy. The most noted example was the slew of new financial products (e.g., CDOs, credit default swaps, etc.) in the late 1990s and 2000s—innovations (new types of services and related business models) that served the interests of the developers of them at the expense of the rest of us. But overall, innovations—in the form of better machines, improved medicines, new ways of communicating and even new technology-enabled business models like Uber and online commerce—are progressive in nature, leading to a better life for most people.

Despite this, many progressives are troubled by innovations like Uber and Amazon that lead to creative destruction (e.g., taking jobs from taxi drivers, and putting family-owned bookstores out of business) because they place greater emphasis on the welfare of the workers who suffer from destruction than they do on the beneficiaries of the creative technological innovation (e.g., consumers of the new and/or cheaper products and services, and new firms developing them and their workers).

But all too often going slowly by resisting these innovations means protecting businesses and professionalised guilds—such as real estate agents, professors, lawyers and doctors—that profit handsomely from stasis. As economist Joseph Schumpeter wrote, "The resistance which comes from interests threatened by an innovation in the productive process is not likely to die out as long as the capitalist order persists." All too often these interests are able to enlist progressives to their cause by telling a tale that their self-preservation is in the interest of workers and consumers or as in the case of small businesses, to assert that they are in solidarity with workers against large capitalist enterprises. But small businesses are in it to make a profit and are more than happy to keep large profits when times are good, all the while usually paying their workers less than large corporations.

We see this attempt to portray business or professional class self-interest as being aligned with the public interest in the current European opposition to US technology companies. For example, Mathias Döpfner, the CEO of the German media group Axel Springer, wrote in an open letter to Google executive chairman Eric Schmidt, that "Google is sitting on the entire current data trove of humanity like the giant Fáfner in The Ring of the Nibelung". Of course, what he failed to mention is that Axel Springer is in competition with Google. Dopfner was simply trying to use government to protect his business interests, as any good CEO should do. But it does not mean that progressives have to go along with it. In most cases, by siding with incumbents—big or small—seeking protection from creative destruction, progressives are siding with slower economic growth and innovation. And that will only mean lower wage growth, fewer good jobs and reduced public revenues to support progressive goals of a sustained, if not broadened, delivery of public goods.

But hasn't Thomas Piketty's *Capital in the Twenty-First Century* shown us that technological innovation and productivity no longer benefit working people, and accrue largely to the Mathias Döpfners of the world? If this is actually the case, then creative destruction is destructive for most of us and creative for only a few wealthy winners. In fact, as Stephen Rose shows in a new ITIF report "Was JFK wrong? Does Rising Productivity No Longer Lead to Substantial Middle Class Income Gains?" newly released data from the US Congressional Budget Office show that the bottom 90 per cent of American households got not the nine per cent of income growth Piketty found but between 54 and 59 per cent of growth. This means that the bottom 90 per cent of Americans still did not get their proportional share of growth and thus income inequality rose. But it would be a mistake for progressives to conclude that they did not benefit substantially from productivity growth and innovation in the form of more and better technology (e.g., computers, cell phones, broadband internet etc.), longer lives, bigger and better equipped homes, and more recreational options.

As a result, "going slowly" means growing slowly for not just the economy but most households. The reality is that economic progress is not possible without the kind of disruption that technological innovation engenders. The job of progressives should not be a populist one of resisting creative destruction, but a progressive one of enabling innovation and helping those workers hurt by creative destruction to adapt, including by more progressive taxation.

Many progressives will deny this characterisation and assert that they are in fact pro-innovation. But all too often that translates into support for only a particular kind of innovation; the kind that is only creative and not destructive. Indeed, few progressives would oppose Philips opening up a new factory in Amsterdam to make semiconductors or a startup firm in Paris coming up with a new cool consumer device. But when it comes to innovation that might disrupt other businesses and business models the support becomes more tentative, often turning to opposition. A case in point was when the German economy minister Sigmar Gabriel called Amazon, Apple, Facebook and Google "brutal information capitalism" saying "Either we defend our freedom and change our policies, or we become digitally hypnotised subjects of a digital rulership."

Innovation that improves living standards and quality of life—long the key goal of progressives—is more than just some cool new technology. It is about constant transformation of an economy and its institutions. But progressives have an ambiguous relationship with constant transformation, especially if it has the potential to upset the delicate balance of social democratic societies.

However, many visionaries are working to convince fellow European progressives of the need to embrace creative destruction coupled with progressive policies to ensure more benefit from it. Paul Giacobbi, a member of the French Assembly, states: "The idea that nothing will change, no factory will ever close, and restructuring will not be a permanent feature is contrary to everything that the direction of the world tells us every day." Unless progressives can accept that innovation entails plant closures and job losses, new technologies with uncertain social or environmental impacts, and new kinds of business models and organisations, then they will fail at their central task of improving life for working Europeans.

This does not mean abandoning workers and consumers to the vagaries of market capitalism and globalisation. But it does mean embracing innovation—the wellspring of that "gale of creative destruction" of which Schumpeter wrote—because enables needed productivity improvements and the dynamic creation of new firms or activities that create new value.

Robert Atkinson is the founder and president of the Information Technology and Innovation Foundation, a Washington, DC-based policy thinktank

I

Jobs, Living Standards and Well-Being

TRANSLATING INNOVATION INTO INCREASES IN LIVING STANDARDS

Andrew Sharpe

In principle, innovation spurs productivity growth, which leads to rising incomes and living standards. In practice, this relationship is not quite so simple. The linkage, or nexus, between innovation and productivity and living standards is by no means automatic. There are significant measurement issues, and the relationship between productivity and real wages is complex. However, policies can help to tighten the relationship between innovation and broad-based improvements in living standards.[1]

UNDERESTIMATING INCREASES IN LIVING STANDARDS

Innovations are very diverse in nature and range greatly in their impact on well-being and consumer welfare. Innovations have traditionally been divided into process innovations that reduce costs in the production process and product innovations that change the nature of the product consumed or develop new goods or services. The impact of process innovations on productivity and living standards is relatively straightforward. Process innovations reduce costs and,

in competitive markets, prices fall. These price declines are captured in a lower rate of growth (or absolute fall) in the Consumer
Price Index. For a given gain in nominal wages or incomes, the
population is better off in real terms.

The impact of product innovation, which results in improved or
new products, on measured living standards must also pass through
changes in prices indices. But there is a problem. Improvements in
product quality, and even more so the appearance of new products,
are not captured in price indices. To be sure, statistical offices have
a long history of attempting to adjust prices for quality, starting with
the automobile and continuing with computers. But many economists feel that these adjustments are grossly inadequate, especially
for new products. And consequently, official data greatly underesti-
mate real improvements in living standards. Indeed, William Nordhaus from Yale University writes:

> During periods of major technological change, the construction
> of price indexes that capture the impact of new technologies on
> living standards is beyond the practical capability of official sta-
> tistical agencies. The essential difficulty arises from the obvious
> but usually overlooked reason that most of the goods consumed
> today were not produced a century ago.[2]

Nordhaus points out that the standard methodology for measuring
prices captures small changes but misses the revolutionary improvements in economic life. These measures overstate price growth because they may not capture quality changes; they measure the price
of goods and services but do not capture the change in efficiency of
these goods and services; and they do not capture the enormous
change in the efficiency of delivery of goods and services when new
products are introduced.

Nordhaus estimates that 37 per cent of output is in tectonically
shifting sectors. In these sectors, such as medical care, household
appliances, electronics, communications, and transportation, change
in production and consumption is so vast that price indices do not
attempt to capture qualitative changes. An additional 36 per cent of

output is in seismically active sectors, such as housing, where there have been major changes but goods and services are still recognisably similar to their counterparts in earlier periods. The remaining 27 per cent of output is produced in run-of-the- mill sectors, like food and clothing, where changes in technology have been small.

Based on his estimates of the price of light, Nordhaus develops low- and high-bias scenarios for the three sectors. In the low-bias scenario he assumes that there is no bias for price indices for the output of run-of-the-mill sectors, 0.5 per cent per year bias for seismically active sectors, and 0.93 per cent bias in tectonically active sectors. In the high-bias scenario the bias assumptions are 0.5, 1.85, and 3.7 per cent respectively. The conventional price indices show that real wages increased at a 1.4 per cent average annual rate in the US from 1800 to 1992, or by a factor of 13. Under the low-bias scenario, Nordhaus finds that real wages increased by 1.9 per cent per year or by a factor of 40; and in the high-bias scenario by 2.8 per cent per year or by a factor of 190.

This underestimation of real wage growth that Nordhaus documented up to 1992 has undoubtedly continued since then. The IT revolution has brought many new products whose contribution to our living standards, not to mention our well-being, is not being adequately captured in official statistics. The smartphone did not exist 20 years ago so it was not part of the price index for communications at the time. This means that the price of smartphones was not included in the price index until the Consumer Price Index basket was updated for new types of consumer expenditure. More importantly, the services provided by a smartphone are not comparable in many ways to those of a traditional telephone. The measurement issues surrounding these "new goods" apply to the systems of national accounts in all countries.

This example can be multiplied many times over. The introduction of email services, such as Gmail, made it possible to easily access one's email account anywhere in the world—a highly valued service that consumers do not even have to pay for. The world wide web provides instant access to massive amounts of information. Consumers enjoy greater reliability and convenience from app-based taxi firms such as Uber even if the actual prices of taxi or "personal transportation" services are unchanged. Just as official price series did not capture quality improvements in the price of light arising from the innovation of electricity in the nineteenth and twentieth centuries, in the twenty-first century official price series are not capturing the benefits for human welfare from the IT revolution.

This underestimation of advances in living standards in official statistics does not, however, diminish the existence of social problems. The objective world would not be any different if statistical agencies published data showing that real wages had been growing rapidly instead of stagnating, although perceptions of the world may change. There would still be unemployment, poverty in a relative sense, income inequality, and economic insecurity. Even with the benefits of the IT revolution captured in our economic statistics, the current unequal sharing of the benefits of innovation and productivity growth would be unchanged.

But measurement is important for at least two reasons. First, perceptions of progress matter. In *The Moral Consequences of Economic Growth* Benjamin Freidman demonstrated that rising incomes lead to more open and democratic societies, and that the loss of a sense of "getting ahead" can lead to rigidity and intolerance.[3] If, based on inadequate official statistics, the population believes that living standards are not rising when progress is actually taking place, the benefits of rising incomes may not be fully realised. Second, better metrics would shed light on the performance of countries on key economic variables, such as innovation and productivity.

THE PRODUCTIVITY-WAGES NEXUS

The benefits of innovation, especially process innovation, and productivity are delivered to workers through their wages, which rise with labour productivity growth under competitive markets. But labour productivity gains do not automatically translate into wage increases for the median worker for several reasons. From a technical perspective, the growth rate of the GDP deflator, which is used to deflate nominal output to obtain real output and productivity measures, may differ from that of the Consumer Price Index, which is used to deflate nominal wages to obtain real wages. This is often referred to as labour's "terms of trade". Second, and more important from a social or equity perspective, the share of labour in nominal national income may fall and the share of capital income rise. Third, among recepients of labour income, increased wage inequality can drive a wedge between the advance in median and average wage productivity growth. Indeed, much of the income of the top one per cent is derived from work and the rising income share of this group has contributed to the increased gap between productivity and median wages.

A number of studies have documented the failure of real wages to track labour productivity growth. For example:

- In the US, labour productivity increased by 80 per cent between 1973 and 2011, while median real hourly wages remained virtually stagnant.[4]
- In Canada, labour productivity rose 37 per cent between 1980 and 2005, yet median real earnings exhibited no increase.[5]
- In the UK, in the 1972–2010 period labour productivity grew 42 per cent faster than the median wage.[6]

The main proximate explanation for lagging median wages is increased wage inequality as labour compensation at the upper end of the wage distribution—both the top 10 per cent and the top one per cent—has seen much more rapid growth than elsewhere in the distribution. In addition, the share of labour income in GDP has also fallen in many countries. A more fundamental explanation for these developments is the weakening bargaining power of workers in the bottom half of the wage distribution due to high unemployment and labour underutilisation. This is a consequence of the weak macro economy, globalisation and competition from low wage countries, and skill-biased technical change. Other factors that have heightened wage inequality include "winner take all" compensation schemes and large increases in CEO compensation, in part reflecting deficiencies in corporate governance practices.

POLICIES TO SHARE THE WEALTH

Given the role of wages in the distribution of the benefits of innovation, the key to ensure not only that policies maximise growth, but that the benefits from that growth are broadly distributed over time is that all workers receive wage increases commensurate with average productivity gains. A variety of policies can be developed to attain this objective. More stimulative macroeconomic policies, especially fiscal policies, can produce a tighter labour market. The increased demand for labour raises the proportion of the population with a job, and hence more people have wage income allowing them to enjoy the new products that innovation has brought forward. The tighter labour market also increases the bargaining power of workers, thereby boosting wage growth. Restrictive monetary policies based on a fear of inflation have the opposite effects and can increase income inequality.

Specific policies that raise wages at the lower end of the wage distribution are also needed. Both wages subsidies to low-wage workers and higher minimum wages are policies that should be considered to boost the income of the poorly paid and ensure that they benefit from innovation. An additional benefit of higher minimum wages is that it can lead to higher labour productivity growth as firms have a greater incentive to substitute capital for labour.

The IT revolution is making the world a richer and more interesting place to live. Our statistical system is inadequate to capture the impacts of these revolutionary technological developments on our standard of living. Compared to the past we are much better off than we realise. But despite these measurement issues, the sharing of the gains from innovation have been very unequal, as seen by the growing gap between labour productivity and median wages. Policies are needed to boost the incomes of those in the bottom half of the income distribution.

Andrew Sharpe is founder and executive director of the Ottawa-based Centre for the Study of Living Standards (CSLS)

NOTES

1. Aggregate living standards are defined simply as Gross Domestic Product (GDP) or Gross Domestic Income (GDI) per capita and are not meant to be a measure of welfare or well-being.

2. William Nordhaus, "Do Real Wage and Real Output Measures Capture Reality: the history of lighting Suggest Not," *Cowles Foundation Paper,* No. 957, 1998, p. 29: http://dido.wss.yale.edu/P/cp/p09b/p0957.pdf.

3. Benjamin Friedman, *The Moral Consequences of Economic Growth* (New York, Alfred Knopf, 2006).

4. Lawrence Mishel and Kar-Fai Gee, "Why Aren't Workers Benefiting from Productivity Growth in the US*?" International Productivity Monitor*, Number 23, Spring, 2012, pp. 31–43, http://www.csls.ca/ipm/23/IPM-23-Mishel-Gee.pdf. For a very useful detailed analysis of income measurement issues that that finds stronger median income growth in the US, see Stephen J. Rose, "JFK Was Not Wrong: Rising Productivity Still Leads to Substantial Middle Class Income Gains?" *Information Technology and Innovation Foundation*, December 2014.

5. Andrew Sharpe, Jean-Francois Arsenault and Peter Harrison, "Why Have Real Wags Lagged Productivity Growth in Canada?" *International Productivity Monitor*, Number 17, Fall 2008, pp. 16–27, http://www.csls.ca/ipm/17/IPM-17-sharpe.pdf.

6. J. P. Pessoa and J. van Reenen, "Decoupling of Wage Growth and Productivity Growth? Myth and Reality," *Resolution Foundation*, 2012, http://www.livingstandards.org/wp-content/uploads/2012/02/Decoupling-of-wages-and-productivity.pdf.

GOOD JOBS IN AN ERA OF TECHNOLOGICAL DISRUPTION

Matthew Whittaker

There are very few economists who would speak out against technological development as being a force for good. Innovation and gains in productivity are central to boosting incomes, feeding into a virtuous cycle in which rising aggregate demand fuels employment growth which, in turn, pushes incomes higher still. It is true that the initial benefits are likely to be unevenly shared and that the process of creative destruction can generate short-term disruption, but the aggregate gains outweigh the losses and are expected, over time, to be recycled and redistributed.

And yet the dominant narrative of recent years has emphasised the negative impact of the latest wave of technological change on the incomes and job prospects of ordinary workers across advanced economies. The virtuous cycle appears to have been broken as income growth has slowed for the masses. Gains have become too concentrated, with there being too few winners to generate the volume of spending, investing or state-directed redistribution required to cascade wealth through society.

Central to this argument is the claim that we are in the midst of a "hollowing out" of middle-skilled jobs. The theory goes that new technology is enabling higher-skilled workers to be more productive, while ever more powerful and cheaper machines are increasingly taking on the tasks carried out by those in the middle—from car assembly to book-keeping and secretarial roles. The technological revolution is less relevant for some lower-skilled jobs such as caring and cleaning, with demand for such workers continuing to rise. Across a range of mature economies, studies have found evidence to support the idea that employment is becoming more polarised.

So, while technological change is clearly providing opportunities for some, it appears to be making life harder for others. The reduction of middle-skilled roles is fuelling competition for what Alan Manning terms "lousy" jobs,[1] putting downward pressure on some wages, affecting job security and reducing satisfaction.

In the face of such techno-pessimisms, often the most hopeful account that is mustered is that the benefits associated with new technological waves always feed through to the masses in the end. But it took decades for wages to start matching productivity gains following the industrial revolution.[2] Must we really resign ourselves to decades of disruption before we can again enjoy steady wage growth?

TECHNO-FATALISM

Techno-fatalism should be eschewed, not least because the case against technology might have been overstated. Look again at the studies of hollowing out and it becomes clear that definitive conclusions are hard to draw. The studies work by ranking occupations in terms of the pay received in an initial period and then measuring employment change in each group over time. This means that no account can be given to new roles that surface during the interim—in the middle and elsewhere—perhaps in reaction to technological change. It also fails to capture any change in the nature of the selected occupational categories over time. This matters because some studies have suggested that job title inflation means that middle-skilled jobs are now masquerading as high-skilled ones.[3]

If technology really is driving hollowing out, it is not clear why the process appeared to pause in the UK, for example, in the pre-crisis years—the very point at which pay growth slowed for many workers—before taking off again in the post-recession period.[4] The timing suggests that other forces have been at play.

So, technology may form part of the explanation for the stagnation in median pay that some argue has haunted the US since the 1970s and other countries in more recent decades, but it is only one driver. The good news is that there is much we can do to tackle some of the other causes.

Change in our industrial mix has been a key contributor. As a sector, manufacturing tends to reward workers well, in a relatively even way and with regularly-spaced opportunities to rise up the career (and pay) ladder. Contraction in this part of the economy, contrasts with growth in services, leading to more polarised outcomes. Employment has risen in relatively low-paying industries such as retail and hospitality and in high-paying ones such as business services and finance. The latter sector in particular produces disproportionate rewards for professionals, owners and shareholders rather than workers, and is marked by very uneven distribution of pay. Of course this industrial evolution is connected to technological developments and there are global drivers including Chinese exchange rate policy and other mercantilist policies, but there were clear domestic political decisions behind the drive to deregulate financial services and our growing deference to the shareholder.

Look to countries such as Sweden and Denmark where technological pressures are no less acute than in the UK or the US yet pay distributions appear much more even. Why? In part, it stems from cultural differences regarding pay differentials; in part, we can point to the role of collective bargaining, better relations between employers and employees and state intervention in the labour market.

And of course technological advancement benefits consumers, by introducing new products, reducing costs and making transactions easier, thereby alleviating pressure on wages. To the extent that it reduces bureaucratic and fixed costs associated with setting up a business, it can also help to democratise entrepreneurialism.

Taken in the round, technological trends remain something to be celebrated. That is not to say that there are not difficulties associated with innovation. Again though, we are far from powerless to mitigate these effects.

SHARING IN THE SUCCESS OF TECHNOLOGICAL CHANGE

The most obvious focus for policy is education. During the industrial revolution, it was the extension of education that was credited with finally facilitating the transference of productivity gains into wage growth. Clearly, in today's world of universal attendance, similar gains will be harder to achieve. But there is still much scope for boosting participation in further (often referred to in the US as "continuing") and higher education. And it is not just participation that matters, but the content and quality of schooling. Old skills are set to become obsolete—who needs rote learning when we have hand-held devices with encyclopaedic knowledge?—while programming, logic and the softer skills that robots will find harder to master will become ever-more valuable.

Of course, educational plans take time to bear fruit and can fall victim to the short-termism of politics. Building consensus will be an important part of the process. And we should not give up on today's generation of workers: re-training opportunities should be extended to adults in order to allow them to keep up with the pace of change. Technology itself can play its part in delivering this new form of learning in ever more efficient and accessible ways.

More immediately, combatting the concentration of gains from today's growth in the hands of a relatively small collection of owners and high earners is likely to require a reassessment of the adequacy of our tax and benefit policies. If the gains from today's growth are not being shared sufficiently through normal market mechanisms, then there is a clear case for directed redistribution instead.

If, for example, the pattern of the industrial revolution is repeated, in which the capital share of GDP gains rises while the labour share falls, then we will need a new focus on wealth taxation. Indeed, the fact that wealth inequality already dwarfs income inequality means that such a focus is likely to be one worth pursuing in any event.

For workers at the lower end of the earnings distribution, more might be done through the use of in-work support measures such as tax credits or through a renewed focus on higher minimum wages. The idea that we should increase the cost of labour in this way at a time when we are already worried about capital substitution will strike some as perverse. Yet the evidence base showing how minimum wages have supported workers and reduced inequality without costing jobs is very much stronger than the one pointing to an imminent rise of the robots.

The bolder the approach, the larger the trade-offs. But a policy of deliberately destroying the least attractive and lowest paid jobs has clear upsides—as long as displaced workers can find new opportunities. By utilising technological developments to automate unpleasant and poorly remunerated tasks while simultaneously boosting the productive potential of lower skilled workers, the transition from a low-pay to a higher-pay economy can be smoothed.

There appears to be a growing consensus around many of these approaches. Improving educational outcomes is entirely non-controversial, while redistribution and support for low paid workers is being championed across the political spectrum. What is lacking to date is a focus on demand: which sectors will be the creators of good, middle income jobs of the future?

The most obvious candidate is caring. Populations are ageing and it is hard to envisage robots meeting this particular need. But funding for care services is already stretched and there is an apparent lack of public appetite to rectify this—through either private or public financing. In the absence of a radical shift in position, can the caring sector really expand employment in a significant way? Even if it can, other sectors will need to develop as well. Identifying and supporting these areas of labour demand should be forming a natural complement to the current focus on labour supply. The lack of activity in this area so far is a cause for concern.

TECHNOLOGICAL CHANGE AND GOOD JOBS

Technology and innovation undoubtedly enhance everyday life, but the current phase of development is concentrating these gains too tightly. As before, society is likely to find a way of working with this changing environment to spread the benefits more widely. But it is not enough to sit tight and wait for this to happen of its own accord. The challenge for progressives in the coming years is to proactively mould labour supply and demand in order to ensure that technological change produces good jobs for the many rather than the few.

Matthew Whittaker is chief economist at The Resolution Foundation, London

NOTES

1. Alan Manning, "Lovely and Lousy Jobs", *CentrePiece*, LSE, Autumn 2013

2. Speaking in 1871, John Stuart Mill argued that the industrial revolution had not yet had much impact, while the economic historian Brad DeLong has suggested that real working class wages were growing by 0.4 per cent a year between 1800 and 1870—faster than in the eighteenth century, but modest nonetheless. Average annual growth jumped to 1.2 per cent between 1870 and 1950 and two per cent in the post-war years. See, for example, Bradford DeLong, "Lighting the Rocket of Growth and Lightening the Toil of Work", *Grasping Reality blog*, 3 September 2013

3. Craig Holmes and Ken Mayhew, "The Changing Shape of the UK Job Market and its Implications for the Bottom Half of Earners", *Resolution Foundation*, March 2012

4. J. P. Pessoa and James Plunkett, "A Polarising Crisis? The Changing Shape of the UK and US Labour Markets from 2008 to 2012", *Resolution Foundation*, 2013

THE PROMISE OF DATA INNOVATION

Daniel Castro

Data-driven innovation has the potential to be a major part of the European effort to grow the economy. In addition, data is at the heart of many initiatives that will have a substantial positive impact on the welfare of individuals and communities, such as to improve healthcare and education. However, these opportunities will not be fully realised unless European policymakers embrace the potential of data driven innovation. Going forward, European leaders should focus on creating policies that enable data to be shared and reused throughout the economy so as to maximise the benefits of data.

THE DATA ECONOMY

When it comes to the economy, if Europe hopes to close the productivity gap that has steadily widened since 1995 between itself and the US, it should look to greater adoption of information technology (IT).[1] Unfortunately many European policymakers have focused more on how to grow their own domestic IT services sector, including through efforts such as building a "European Cloud", rather than on promoting the use of the technology itself in established industries. However, European policymakers should worry less about building the infrastructure to store and process data, and more about how to extract insights from these data sets.

European policymakers do not need to look abroad to see the positive impact of data. By all accounts, the potential economic impact of big data in Europe is substantial. The McKinsey Global Institute, for example, estimates that big data can save the public sector alone more than €100bn in operational efficiency improvements.[2] Today, many of Europe's top companies are investing in big data analytics to stay competitive in the global economy. For example, Royal Dutch Shell has partnered with companies like IBM, HP and Dreamworks to use data, sensors, and advanced visualisations to explore thousands of oil wells; retail giant Tesco uses in-store sensors and predictive modeling to optimise the heating, cooling, and refrigeration systems in its stores to cut costs and prevent spoilage; and the Dutch bank ING leverages technologies like cloud computing to integrate huge data streams from its website, call centres, and online user feedback to derive new customer insights. And for some companies the challenge is less about acquiring technology, and more about how to leverage the technology in place. As Volkswagen CEO Martin Winterkorn has noted, "Our cars are already mobile computer centres, with 1.5 km of cables, more than 50 control units, and the computing power of 20 highly advanced PCs."[3]

QUALITY OF LIFE

In addition to economic improvement, there are a growing number of opportunities to use data and analytics to improve quality of life for citizens and address important social issues such as healthcare and education.

Healthcare

With an ageing population set to increase demand for healthcare, Europe faces mounting pressure to improve the effectiveness and efficiency of its healthcare system. European policymakers should look to data as a tool to radically improve healthcare quality and bring down costs. Data is being used today to do everything from developing new drugs to delivering care to patients, and public health officials can use better data to improve disease surveillance and help prevent the spread of communicable diseases. Healthcare providers are also leveraging data in electronic health records to improve diagnostics and clinical decisions for patients, and medical researchers are analysing clinical trial data and genomic data to identify new treatments tailored for specific populations and unlocking the promise of personalised medicine. For example, pharmaceutical company Pfizer used its advanced data capabilities to develop a drug for a specific type of lung cancer associated with a gene mutation, and the European Medicines Agency granted it conditional approval.[4] These types of advances are only possible because increases in computing power have dramatically lowered the price of using data in healthcare. While it took the Human Genome Project $3bn and 10 years to sequence the first human genome, companies are now able to do this in a matter of hours for less than $1,000.[5]

Wearables and other connected devices offer another opportunity to use data to modernise healthcare. Activity trackers, such as those offered by FitBit, Jawbone, and Nike, can be used to improve personal fitness by monitoring individuals' progress, encouraging them to complete their goals, and providing incentives such as discounts to keep individuals motivated. These devices can also help patients obtain better healthcare outcomes. Healthcare providers can also use wearables and connected devices to offer patients better remote monitoring services in their own homes. These types of services not only give individuals greater independence, but they also keep them out of the hospital thereby cutting costs. For example, patients can use smart pill bottles to receive automatic reminders so they do not forget to take their medicine. These types of interventions, while seemingly small, can have a major impact: 50 per cent of Europeans do not take their medication as prescribed and reducing non-adherence could save Europe €125bn annually and reduce premature deaths by 200,000 per year.[6]

Education

Data stands ready to disrupt the education sector. Just as data can be used to create personalised medicine, data can be used to deliver personalised education, build more efficient schools, and help students and their parents make better decisions about their education.

By making better use of data and analytics, educators can tailor lessons to students' specific learning styles and allow students to learn at their own pace. Schools can use adaptive learning software with integrated analytics to assess student performance and then spend more time focused on each student's individual needs. Educators can link this data to other school records, including classroom behaviour, to better monitor their classrooms, intervene when problems arise earlier, and create custom learning plans. A number of European schools are beginning to provide their teachers with tools like learning analytics software and online dashboards so they can use data to improve their teaching methods.[7]

Data can also be used to create more efficient public schools, as well as lead to improvements in higher education. Schools are using data to help reduce dropout rates by intervening sooner when students are at risk. Colleges and universities are using data mining techniques to process a multitude of data points, such as the number of times students check in to the library and how often they log into virtual classrooms, to predict student achievement. For example, Manchester Metropolitan University and Leeds Metropolitan University in the UK use analytics to help improve their retention rate.[8]

Finally, students and their parents can make better decisions about their education, such as where to go to school or what to study, using better data that helps predict both costs and future earnings. These types of tools can help ensure students obtain the skills demanded by employers and ensure that Europe has a competitive workforce with the skills needed to compete in a global economy.

A TWENTY-FIRST CENTURY APPROACH TO REGULATING TECHNOLOGY

Better use of data helps drive improvements in efficiency, better decisions, and more rational investment. Given their importance to people's lives and livelihoods, hospitals and schools should be the first place data is used, not the last. As European policymakers work to grow the economy and address major social issues, they should consider carefully the role of data in achieving these ends. Doing so will not only require bold government leadership to promote the adoption of data-related technologies in industries like healthcare and education, as well as public education about the benefits, it will also require rethinking policies that impact how data is allowed to be used.

Both the rapid pace of technological progress and competition from global peers means that regulations which inadvertently slow down innovation will have an outsized impact on the economy as other countries take the lead. In particular, European policymakers should move away from a "privacy at all costs" mentality that restricts data flows both between organisations and across borders. Instead, Europe should embrace a twenty-first century approach to regulating technology that encourages beneficial applications while narrowly targeting rules to address specific consumer harms. Importantly, this will require rethinking existing data regulations, as well as new proposals such as the General Data Protection Regulations, which can have a chilling effect on the use of data, and instead supporting an environment that encourages sharing and reuse of data.[9] Long-term, the goal of European policymakers should be to actively work to promote the use of data and maximise its potential benefits. Doing so will allow Europe to better address its most pressing challenges, as well as position itself to better compete in the global economy.

Daniel Castro is director of the Center for Data Innovation, Washington, DC

NOTES

1. Ben Miller and Rob Atkinson, "Raising European Productivity Through ICT," June 2014, *Information Technology and Innovation Foundation*, http://www2.itif.org/2014-raising-eu-productivity-growth-ict.pdf.

2. James Manyika et al., "Big Data: The Next Frontier for Innovation, Competition, and Productivity," *McKinsey Global Institute*, May 2011, http://www.mckinsey.com/insights/business_technology/big_data_the_ next_frontier_for_innovation.

3. Christine Tierney, "VW CEO: Yes To Big Data, No To Big Brother," *Forbes*, March 9, 2014, http://www.forbes.com/sites/christinentierney/ 2014/03/09/vw-ceo-yes-to-big-data-no-to-big-brother/.

4. European Medicines Agency, "Xalkori," July 5, 2014, http://www. ema.europa.eu/docs/en_GB/document_library/EPAR_-_Summary_for_ the_public/human/002489/WC500134762.pdf.

5. Robbie Gonzalez, "Breakthrough: Now We Can Sequence a Human Genome for Just $1000," *io9*, January 15, 2014: http://io9.com/ breakthrough-now-we-can-sequence-a-human-genome-for-ju-1502081435.

6. European Federation of Pharmaceutical Industries and Associations, "Patient adherence," http://www.efpia.eu/topics/people-health/patient-adherence.

7. European Commission, "The NMC Horizon Report Europe: 2014 Schools Edition," 2014, http://cdn.nmc.org/media/2014-nmc-horizon-report-EU-EN.pdf.

8. Ruth Drysdale, "University Data Can Be a Force for Good," *The Guardian*, November 27, 2013, http://www.theguardian.com/higher-education-network/blog/2013/nov/27/university-data-student-engagement-retention.

9. Travis Korte, "Proposed EU Data Protection Regulations Could Impede Medical Research," *Center for Data Innovation*, October 21, 2014,

http://www.datainnovation.org/2014/10/proposed-eu-data-protection-regulations-could-impede-medical-research/.

THE INTERNET IS AN ENGINE FOR EUROPEAN GROWTH

Matt Brittin

For many today, the internet provides new opportunities to create a new business, generate an income, and enjoy more consumer choice and a more fulfilling way of life. For others, the internet symbolises the broad changes society faces: the end of job stability, and the rise of freelancing, self-employment and odd-jobs. These changes also create uncertainty and worry. But the outlook can be very positive for individuals and for the economy as a whole.

In fact, the internet is a powerful engine of growth across Europe. It serves as a platform from which economic activity of all kinds is creating new opportunities for individuals, businesses and government to respond to changing consumer behaviour and economic patterns. Digital technology enables entrepreneurs to start a business and succeed online, as well as reach customers, cut costs and scale across the world. Digital technology is expanding the size of the economic pie rather than creating a zero sum game of winners and losers.

NEW OPPORTUNITIES

Indeed, the rise of e-commerce and online trading is generating significant economic returns and driving a positive online trade balance for many countries. Researchers at OC&C found that the UK could see its e-commerce exports grow by £32bn, from £13bn in 2013 to an expected £45bn in 2020.[1] This already creates an online trade balance of $1bn, supporting economic growth. The most recent Christmas shopping season broke new records in online shopping, with consumers increasingly trusting the internet as a place to buy and retailers of all sizes able to find their customers around the world.

The move to online shopping underscores a real change in the opportunities for entrepreneurs. This goes beyond e-commerce, as the rise of European startup hubs demonstrate. I am constantly impressed by the East London startup scene that has become the envy of the world. It rivals New York as a centre for financial technology innovation. And London is not alone in Europe in developing cutting edge talent and ideas. World beating consumer apps and impressive business solutions are being created across Europe in cities like Berlin, Amsterdam, Paris and Stockholm. These are just a few of the thriving hubs of innovation where digital technology breaks down barriers to new business creation and growth.

Focusing on young, growing business is not only exciting, but it makes good economic sense too. We know that these new businesses create real and lasting impact on the economy. Research from Nesta and the OECD shows that it is new businesses that are driving growth in employment and gross value added. The OECD found that companies that are older than five years reduced employment every year between 2001 and 2011, while companies under five years old were net job creators in the same period.[2] This research indicates that we should be supporting the young, dynamic companies that drive job growth.

BENEFITTING SOCIETY

Critically, the positive economic value is seen not only in the macroeconomic data but in the outcomes for individuals too. The UK-based RSA found that the rise of self-employment, facilitated in part by digital technology, is creating positive outcomes for workers. In a survey of the self-employed, 84 per cent said they were more content being self-employed than working for a company, 82 per cent said the work they do is more meaningful and 87 per cent that they have more freedom to do the things they want. The RSA also found that the growth in self-employment predates the economic downturn.[3] This shatters the myth that the self-employed have been forced into their situation because of economic disruption and are scraping to make ends meet.

Building on this research, Google commissioned Kitty Ussher, former chief secretary to the UK treasury and an economist by trade, to examine the impact of the internet on social mobility in the UK. Her research shows that online trading creates new opportunities for traditionally vulnerable individuals and families. She found that selling goods online is a source of income for families regardless of their educational attainment. People who never went beyond basic qualifications are often earning high incomes through online selling and they are aware that setting up an online business has fewer risks than building a traditional business.[4]

We see these examples everyday as small businesses use our platforms as an engine for their growth. Take Julie Dean as just one example. Back in 2008, Julie started making handcrafted leather satchels from her kitchen table. She was looking to pay for her girls' school fees and to balance her role as a mother. She drove interest in her Cambridge Satchels website through Google tools and has grown her small business into a multi-million pound company, launching her first bricks and mortar shop in 2013, and creating product tie-ups with some of fashion's biggest names. Julie's success shows this opportunity is real.

EUROPE'S DIGITAL IMPERATIVE

For policymakers looking to create a balanced, growing economy, the question is what more can be done to enable more Julies to succeed and ensure that businesses across the economy can take advantage of digital technology. There are three areas that we see as critical to unlocking this opportunity: "permissionless innovation", completing the digital single market and boosting digital skills.

Permissionless Innovation

At Google we are often asked by policymakers how they can re-create the dynamism of Silicon Valley in their city or country. While many of the qualities that make Silicon Valley a favoured home for technologists and entrepreneurs are difficult, if not impossible, to replicate. One shift we could make here in Europe is to adopt a bias in favour of new ideas—so-called permissionless innovation.

This is critical to creating an environment where risk-takers, investors and businesses can not only imagine the next big thing, but create it in an environment where society will be open to new ideas. Too often in Europe, bureaucracy and fear of the unknown stand in the way of ingenuity and innovation. This creates an environment where new ideas are less likely to take route and new business models will be squashed by regulation before their full impact can ever be understood.

Completing the Digital Single Market

In addition to shifting our posture towards openness and innovation, we Europeans should also make completing the digital single market a priority over the next five years. The European commission president, Jean-Claude Juncker, has rightly pointed to the huge opportunity for Europe in embracing digital technology and further removing barriers to the trade of digital goods and services.

There are three key areas for the new European commission to pursue in making this longstanding goal a reality. First, the commission should look to create one set of rules, not 28. In too many areas, like data protection, consumer rights and intellectual property, different rules across Europe create obstacles, administrative costs and burdens for small businesses.

Second, Europe must be open to the rest of the world, not closed, so that Europe's 500 million consumers can enjoy the benefits of the web wherever they are accessing it from. Global openness ensures that European consumers have access to the most innovative and compelling online services, and that European businesses grow stronger by competing with the world's best. Openness also means open and fair trading rules for the flow of data, increasing cross-border trade within Europe and adopting a system of taxation that does not ring fence the digital economy by treating it differently to the rest of the economy.

Finally, Europe must support innovation and reject protectionism. Europe needs a positive vision for building the digital economy that promotes a dynamic telecoms market, entrepreneurialism and skills.

Boosting Digital Skills

Building a genuine single digital market will ensure that entrepreneurs from across Europe will be able to benefit from the opportunities that the internet and digital technology are creating. These new opportunities need new kinds of workers with the rights skills to help these businesses grow. It is no secret that employers are increasingly looking for workers with digital skills. Whether they are coders to build the next killer app or marketers who can use digital tools to reach consumers in new ways, these skills are essential and in demand.

We also know that based on current projections there is a growing gap between the skills required and the training that workers receive. The European commission has estimated that there will be one million jobs unfilled in 2020 because of this gap. The risk is that Europe misses out on the potential boom in digital technology as other regions of the world educate talented young people with these skills.

At Google, we believe so strongly in the importance of these skills that we are investing in helping to train hundreds of thousands of people across Europe with digital skills. In Spain, we help young unemployed people to acquire digital marketing skills. In Italy, we have supported young people who help small businesses around the country digitise their companies. And in Germany, we have supported businesses to gain the skills they need to use the web to export and grow.

Over the past six years, economies across Europe have struggled to recover from the worst economic crash in generations. While the internet and digital technology cannot answer all of these challenges, these tools are an engine for economic growth and positive outcomes for people across Europe.

Matt Brittin is the president of Google's business and operations in Europe, the Middle East and Africa

NOTES

1. OC&C, "International eCommerce - the Future is Now: A Study on the International Opportunity for UK Businesses in Today's Disrupted Markets", 2014.

2. OECD, "Young SMEs, Growth and Job Creation", 2014.

3. RSA, "Salvation in a Start-up? The Origins and Nature of the Self-employment Boom", May 2014.

4. Tooley Street Research, "The Effect of the Internet on the Economically Vulnerable", October 2014.

II

Rethinking the Rules of the Game for the Digital Age

UNDERSTANDING AND SHAPING THE COLLABORATIVE ECONOMY

Kathleen Stokes

Did we ever think that ridesharing or timebanks would end up at the top of policymakers' and regulators' agendas? As an increasingly diverse collection of organisations make use of internet technologies to unlock the idling capacity of goods, skills and other useful things, policymakers and the public alike are trying to make sense of this rising trend, and grasp its wider implications.

When Rachel Botsman and Roo Rogers wrote *What's Mine is Ours* in 2010, they predicted that collaborative consumption would emerge as a massive "socioeconomic groundswell".[1] Five years on, many of the examples highlighted by Botsman and Rogers have become household names which have global followings. Collaborative consumption has also evolved to become the collaborative economy, as new collaborative modes of production, finance and learning have steadily emerged.

While collaborative platforms have captured imaginations and gained participants in recent years, many have also prompted court battles, inspired government reviews and even sparked physical altercations. No longer simply nice and niche, collaborative economy organisations and platforms are challenging incumbents and disrupting longstanding approaches to businesses and service provision. Hotels now look at people's spare rooms as potential sources of competition, while a neighbour with spare time may now contend with professionals to undertake odd jobs, like delivering packages or assembling furniture.

Indeed, we have reached a junction in the evolution of the collaborative economy. While efforts to increase awareness and participation have been promising, an abundance of unanswered questions remind us that the collaborative economy is still finding its shape. Building on these initial advances and challenges, the time has come for some longer term thinking about the collaborative economy. To do this, policymakers and the public alike need to recognise the diversity of this emergent space, understand what is actually innovative about different collaborative economy models, and consider what kind of outcomes they want these initiatives to support, or avoid.

COMMON TRAITS, MANY FORMS

In its simplest form, the collaborative economy can be summed up by several key traits: internet technologies are connecting distributed networks of people and goods to make use of idle assets, such as goods, times, skills, space, and finance. Looking across the range of organisations and activities employing these traits, it is pretty clear that the collaborative economy is not a single sector or business model. Community organisations, for example, are using platforms to help people lend and exchange their time, skills and things. Digital startups are establishing successful businesses where peers rent anything from parking spaces, to children's toys, to boats. Local governments are partnering with platforms to offer their assets, such as data, publicly. Even big businesses are backing projects that encourage people to share goods, instead of buying something new. Some of these activities involve money, while others are based on alternative currencies or more altruistic intentions.

However, this diversity is not always apparent. Platforms serving similar functions or operating within the same sector will often be shaped by subtle, but important, differences. Streetbank and eBay, for example, are both online platforms where people can get rid of unwanted things by offering them directly to others. The general purpose of each platform may be similar, but their business models produce both incredibly distinct experiences for users and trajectories for the organisations themselves. eBay has become *the* global market for people to directly sell goods, while Streetbank allows people to give away unwanted goods to neighbours, as its users can only see what is available within a mile of their home.

A COLLABORATIVE ECONOMY—FOR WHAT?

Organisations invariably have different reasons for adopting collaborative models. While some simply see this as a good business opportunity, most founders are also driven by wider aims. When undertaking Nesta's review of the UK collaborative economy,[2] we found four prevailing drivers for initiatives operating within the collaborative economy. Seeing idle assets as an untapped resource, most initiatives are compelled to find ways of creating financial or non-financial value—such as skills for public benefit. More broadly, many organisations are looking to support different types of economic relationships—from alternatives to market-dominant approaches to boosting local economies. Beyond economic drivers, some collaborative economy initiatives also pursue a social aim, or pursue environmental objectives. For instance, a platform may want to improve trust and social capital within communities, or seek to reduce consumption to improve sustainability.

These drivers help us consider why organisations are taking part in the collaborative economy. By understanding what different organisations are working towards, we can also begin to consider the wider implications and possible futures of this diverse field—whether millions of localised economies, a handful of global monopolies, or the normalisation of micro-entrepreneurship.

However, aims alone do not determine the impact of the collaborative economy. To understand the actual effects of the collaborative economy, ambitions and promises must be carefully assessed and evaluated. For example, carsharing schemes which reduce car ownership have the potential to reduce pollution, but not if people begin using cars more frequently than before.

Along with checking claims and assessing whether organisations are meeting their goals, it is also important to consider the unintended consequences of different models and initiatives. These may emerge as collaborative models navigate existing legal and regulatory frameworks, but can also reflect broader socioeconomic conditions. Micro-entrepreneurship platforms may supplement incomes but mass participation could also inadvertently weaken workers' rights and protections. Likewise, long-term tenants already encounter harsher rental markets as more people opt to let out their spare rooms on Airbnb.

Collaborative economy models can encompass a variety of positive or unintended effects. Indeed, given the diversity of collaborative economy initiatives—all the actors, platforms, the sectors affected—finding a single assessment measure or standard is unlikely. Trying to measure the total economic, social or environmental impact of this space is therefore rather difficult and not particularly helpful. Assessing impact at an organisational and sector level will be considerably more useful for understanding whether the collaborative economy is actually reaching its desired outcomes.

LOCATING THE INNOVATION

Along with understanding impact, how can governments and regulators position themselves within the collaborative economy? What should they support (or block) to ensure the greatest possible benefit?

To start, separating out what is new or different about an initiative from "business as usual" can help us to make sense of disruptive and innovative potentials of the collaborative economy. When excited or concerned about an innovation, we can sometimes overhype the exceptionality of the trend. Whether it is access over ownership, distributed networks or digital platforms, nothing in this is particularly new. Online marketplaces and skill-sharing build on the principles of a community noticeboard, while carshare schemes act as distributed alternatives to traditional car rental companies.

However, we see genuine innovation and gains when these traits are applied to more efficient technologies, new business models or unlikely relationships between stakeholders. These differences are particularly important because they have enabled many organisations to become convenient and competitive enough to build considerable followings. Yet the distributed or slightly informal nature of many platforms can rub uncomfortably against existing legal frameworks. For example, when does the exchange of goods or services between neighbours, whether for money or simple reciprocity, become taxable? The answer will depend on existing laws and regulatory frameworks within your jurisdiction—and whether they are being applied in practice.

Some governments have sought to restrict and outlaw such practices, or ignore them when they fall into uncertain or unchartered legal territory. However, retaining the status quo or actively avoiding discrepancies misses the point. The challenges and questions emanating from the collaborative economy are a product of their increasing popularity. With wider participation, different platforms have the potential to reshape our industries, increase productivity, improve collective prosperity, or minimise our ecological footprints.

The choices and organisations we choose to back now will shape the future of the collaborative economy. Many sectors could be disrupted by distinct platforms and organisations. While demand will be a key factor in shaping the collaborative economy, policymakers and regulators can amplify or hinder different models. Effective responses are unlikely to be broad-brush or reactive—instead, a variety of tailored and informed efforts are required.

INCENTIVISING, CHANNELLING AND TESTING INNOVATIONS

How can policymakers ensure this broad array of initiatives fulfils its potential, and avoids some of the earlier traps and challenges? Engaging with the collaborative economy is an important first step. Increasingly, governments at all levels are reviewing existing policies and regulatory frameworks to find ways of accommodating different models within the collaborative economy. By partnering with existing collaborative economy organisations or creating their own initiatives, local governments in the UK like Croydon and Kirklees councils are adopting collaborative models to improve their own public services. And some local governments, like Seoul in South Korea, are creating holistic strategies for the collaborative economy. These link support and funding for promising initiatives, regulatory updates and partnerships to overcome barriers, along with promoting participation within local communities.

Drawing inspiration from these initial efforts, we can also ask what opportunities within the collaborative economy have yet to be explored. When we look across the collaborative economy, many of the fastest growing and most disruptive models operate within a handful of sectors—most notably, transportation, housing, household goods, and informal jobs and tasks. How can innovation be encouraged and incentivised in sectors where collaborative economy models could offer new benefits or extend access. Likewise, rigorous evidence and information on impact is still in short supply. While some platforms have taken steps to measure and demonstrate their impact, policymakers and the public still lack information and guidance on how different initiatives work, and what benefits (and risks) they offer.

Whether you are a policymaker or someone who makes use of collaborative platforms, we need to ask ourselves what we want from the collaborative economy. A clearer sense of our intentions and desired outcomes can help immensely as we look for opportunities to grow, innovate and support the collaborative economy. This can enable it to deliver on its promise and provide the social, environmental and economic benefits we are looking for.

Kathleen Stokes is senior researcher on digital education and the collaborative economy for Nesta, UK

NOTES

1. Rachel Botsman and Roo Rogers, *What's Mine is Ours: The Rise of Collaborative Consumption* (New York: HarperBusiness, 2010), p. xiv

2. Nesta, *Making Sense of the UK Collaborative Economy*, September 2014, http://www.nesta.org.uk/sites/default/files/making_sense_of_the_uk_collaborative_economy_summary_fv.pdf.

INTANGIBLE GOLD: WHY NO RUSH TO FINANCE INNOVATION?

Birgitte Andersen

During the historical gold rush and the American land acquisition period it was economic confidence which allowed finance to flow, industry to unfold, and markets to grow. It was the same during the "black gold" oil boom of the twentieth century. The same could be said for the railways and electrification period. But the new gold is invisible and weightless. It needs a different plan to unlock its value to boost the growth in jobs and welfare we only dream of.

High-growth small and medium sized businesses are key contributors to the regeneration of jobs and economic growth in the twenty-first century. Their growth is boosted by high levels of intellectual capital such as a patent or a great business model. Unfortunately, these "growth stars" seeking resources to scale up their activities and markets face greater difficulties than the rest in accessing growth finance due to their assets being mainly intangible. They may make for riskier investments than buy-to-let property, but they are infinitely more important to our future.

ECONOMIC BOOMS AND THE CRISIS

What matters in today's digital economy are the hard-to-value in-tangibles—computerised algorithms, information, software, big data, patents, copyrights, a great business model, organisational ca-pabilities, social capital, knowledge, skills and strategic networks. Investment in such intangibles and intellectual property (IP) now exceeds that in tangibles such as buildings, machines and raw mate-rials. The UK's annual intangible investment has grown from £50bn to about £140bn between 1990 and today, while it has constantly fluctuated around £80bn for tangibles. The pattern is the same for other developed economies.

We have struck gold. The relative intangible contributions to advanced economies, measured as a proportion of GDP, are today about double that of physical assets. On top of this, the Big Innova-

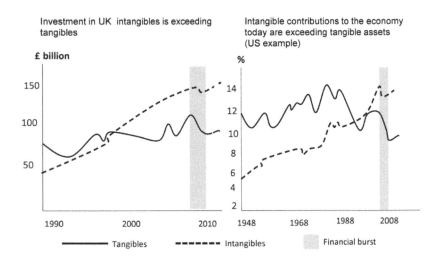

These graphs are schematic illustrations of original sources: Peter Goo-dridge, Jonathan Haskel and Gavin Wallis, "Estimating UK Investment in Intangible Assets", *Nesta Working Paper 14/02*, March 2014; Leonard I. Naka-mura, "Intangible Assets and National Income Accounting: Measuring a Sci-entific Revolution", Working Paper No. 09–11, *Federal Reserve Bank of Phila-delphia*, May 2009.

tion Centre estimates that high-growth firms have 74 per cent more intangible assets and IP on their balance sheet than their slower growing counterparts.[1]

Despite having a significant number of high-growth firms, Britain is still suffering a chronic growth deficit. Investment and growth finance do not back high-growth firms that are capable of scaling their markets and activities. The same can be said for a whole suite of other countries. These are vital elements to be fixed both for the recovery to follow through and for trade deficits to be closed.

But there is plenty of opportunity. We are living through an intangible revolution sparked by computing power and connectivity which can be readily acquired at low and rapidly falling relative cost. There is clear potential for the use of these technologies throughout the economic system: from the way we live, work and run our businesses, to how we spend our leisure time. It is the same story with "big data". Innovation is accelerating with technologies, especially digital ones, which can be applied for general purposes— the internet, visualisation, wireless cables, data mining and sensor technology. The new "smart" societies emerging also address business and societal opportunities for health and life sciences, sustainability and low carbon.

The transformative power of the intangible revolution resembles that of the railways, plastics, electrification, and mass production. Such factors—or more precisely, the way they boosted innovation and investment—spurred a jump in economic activity, productivity and living standards; although typically such improvements were only visible in the long-term. But as productivity growth rates have slumped and unemployment and inequality risen, to boost growth in the twenty-first century we need a much more sophisticated understanding of intangibles across the board, including our institutions that unlock this weightless gold.

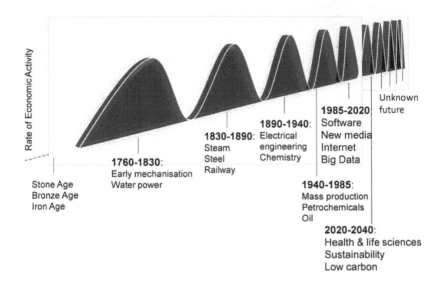

This figure is an updated schematic illustration of the arguments and underpinning research from business cycle academics, such as Joseph Schumpeter (1883–1950), Simon Kuznets (1901–1985) and Christopher Freeman (1921–2010). Original source: Big Innovation Centre.

IT'S THE INTANGIBLE GOLD, STUPID

Europe and Britain both have high-growth firms able to generate the output, jobs and welfare we today only dream of. Unsurprisingly, these are the very same firms that show the strongest signs of innovation, and are rich in IP and intangible assets. Despite the fact that high-growth firms have 74 per cent more intangible assets and intellectual property on their balance sheet than their slower growing counterparts, these firms do not get the support from the financial ecosystem which matches their potential. For example, between 2001 and up to the burst of the financial bubble in 2007 the Big Innovation Centre calculates that the total capital raised in the UK financial system increased by £1,340bn, but investment in innovation and intangible assets over the same period increased by a fraction of this, just £26bn.[2] Moreover, innovative firms are finding it harder to get funding. 57 per cent of innovators had trouble obtaining finance in 2012, up from 38 per cent in 2007.[3]

For high-growth small and medium sized firms the financing problems are especially serious. They are forced to sell off shares far too quickly and cheaply, or have to rely on overdraft lending, which hampers their ability to scale up. Often they sell to foreign companies for all the wrong reasons, at a loss to the economy in the UK case. While bank assets grew to enormous proportions up to the burst of the financial bubble, the economy crunched into debt, unemployment and foreign ownership. Britain is renowned for coming up with great inventions—the jet engine, the computer, the medical scanner and now graphene—but it is other countries and companies that have gone on to exploit them, such as the US or China.

We need our bankers to be as enthusiastic about lending to intangible-rich firms as they are to buy-to-let property companies—today's equivalent of black, or even real, gold. Like gold they offer bankers the seeming watertight security of bricks and mortar, but with the added zest of rising prices and rising rents. In comparison, innovative companies offer little but risk and uncertainty, but they are infinitely more important to our future.

However, unlike a buy-to-let property there is no confident market price for our intangible assets—nor even a well-functioning market. For example, more than half of firms and organisations trading patents in the German pharmaceutical, UK ICT and UK university sectors report that they are not able to assess the degree of novelty of the inventions they trade. This means that they cannot assess the value and true price. Furthermore, half of firms currently active in the open source community, whereby people share ideas openly, have their ideas patented by their co-participants after slight development.[4] This is the abuse of the entrepreneurial commons. We must find ways to more strongly enforce creative commons licences, along with safeguarding technological and inventive solutions with no patents.

Banks do not lend against an asset as collateral that they cannot value, particularly when even the company does not and cannot know how valuable it might be. Hence, we need the alchemy that will turn IP into gold. If the problem could be solved, the returns would be great. The Big Innovation Centre estimates that for any £1m increase in equity finance, high-growth firms co-invest nearly half—£499,000—compared to just £195,000 for all firms.[5]

Large companies know what it means to thrive on their intangible assets and intellectual capital. Today IBM is worth 11 times its book value and Google is worth four times more; and even this valuation is generally regarded as an acute under-estimation. Kraft's generous bid for Cadbury Schweppes and the recent bid by Pfizer for AstraZeneca were about securing all important intangible assets, chiefly their brands and IP pipeline. In 1998, Microsoft was already worth £85.5bn on the market but had a book value of £6.9bn. Even "patent trolls" have emerged with a new controversial business model of "idea grabbing": simply seeking economic rent by enforcing patents against purported infringers without themselves intending to manufacture the patented product or supply the patented service.

For decades, accountants and economists have dumbed down the notion of intangibles to the catch-all term "goodwill", to explain why investors are willing to pay a price that far exceeds companies' book value. In a world in which investment in intangibles now exceeds tangibles that is no longer good enough.

THE NEED FOR AN ENTREPRENEURIAL FINANCE HUB

We need a much more sophisticated understanding of intangibles across the board, including how they are accounted for and how they are valued. Alongside this, we need an entrepreneurial finance ecosystem, or hub, linking high-growth firms with finance providers though IP valuators and IP insurance schemes, which underwrite the value of intangible assets of growing companies. We must also help businesses to understand and communicate the value of their intangible assets and IP, including relationship to cash-flow. In the Big Innovation Centre we are building the Entrepreneurial Finance Hub to do just that.[6] Britain cannot afford anything less, neither can the rest of Europe.

How well do our governments, the EU and regional growth hubs understand this agenda? What are they doing to create an innovation ecosystem which is sufficiently ambitious and supportive? Are our banks, investors, and markets ready?

Birgitte Andersen is chief executive and co-creator of the Big Innovation Centre, London, and runs a thought leadership forum on Intangible Gold.

NOTES

1. H. Sameen and G. Quested, "Disrupted Innovation: Financing innovative small firms in the UK", *Big Innovation Centre*, 2013.

2. H. Sameen, "Two spheres that don't touch", *Big Innovation Centre*, 2013.

3. Lee, N., Sameen, H. and Lloyd, M, "Credit and the Crisis: Access to Finance for Small Innovative Firms", *Big Innovation Centre*, 2013.

4. For example: Andersen, B. and Rossi, F., "Intellectual Assets and Innovation: The SME Dimension". Published in *Intellectual Asset Management: Strategies for Diverse Innovations*, OECD press, 2013, Commissioned by the UK Department for Business, Innovation and Skills.

5. Sameen, H and Quested, G., "Disrupted Innovation: Financing innovative small firms in the UK", *Big Innovation Centre*, 2013.

6. The Entrepreneurial Finance Hub of the Big Innovation Centre was cited in *The Scale-Up Report on UK Economic Growth*, commissioned by UK government and written by Sherry Coutu. Page 67: "Key areas where progress has already been made . . . the Big Innovation Centre's Entrepreneurial Finance Hub will build solutions to finance high-growth firms through the critical phases of growth", iv.

CREATING A CLIMATE FOR DIGITAL ENTREPRENEURS

Desirée van Welsum and Jonathan Murray

The recent arrival of utility-based cloud computing is shifting the focus of the challenge facing digital entrepreneurs from technical barriers to the business environment. This shift reinforces the growing importance of implementing effective policies that foster the best climate for digital service incubation, growth and successful development. Given the critical platform for economic activity that cloud has become it is ever more important that policymakers focus on establishing effective policies that maximise entrepreneurial opportunity. This includes creating an appropriately skilled labour force, ensuring access to investment capital, reducing barriers to creating and growing new businesses and finally ensuring the widest access to cloud-based services for consumers through broadband infrastructure and open trade policies.

Over the last eight years cloud computing has reduced barriers to entry and increased opportunities for digital entrepreneurs. Cloud computing delivers computing services—data storage, computation and networking—to users at the time, to the location, and in the quantity they wish to consume, with costs based only on the resources used. In essence, this transforms the provision of computing resources from a capital investment in fixed infrastructure into a dynamic utility.[1] The "utility" nature of the new cloud computing model means that investment capital that would previously have been needed to build-out dedicated computing infrastructure can now be saved or spent on developing better products or services. The use of cloud computing as the foundation for startups has become so ubiquitous that venture capital firms now routinely refuse to allow investment funds to be spent on fixed computing infrastructure.

The "on-demand" aspect of cloud computing means that the computing costs of delivering a new digital service will be directly proportional to usage of the service by consumers. This enables entrepreneurs to more effectively manage costs and capital utilisation. Cloud computing is inherently "elastic" so costs are only incurred when there is demand. The previous generation of digital entrepreneurs whose services were built on fixed private computing infrastructure fought a constant battle to match the scale of infrastructure investment with user demand. Underinvestment might lead to service quality and availability issues while over-investment often led to inefficient capital utilisation detracting from other critical investments in the business.

Acquiring the specialised expertise—and capital—required to design and implement computing infrastructure which can operate reliably at global scale has been challenging historically. But this capability is now available by default when services are built on top of cloud computing infrastructure. The "global by default" nature of cloud computing based services provides a significant advantage to digital entrepreneurs who wish to scale their services internationally in a short space of time.

In short, the advantages of cloud computing enable digital entrepreneurs to more effectively utilise capital, manage costs, and scale reliably and responsively to growing user demand even when that demand comes from all over the world.

BARRIERS TO DIGITAL ENTREPRENEURSHIP

The main barriers to digital entrepreneurship appear to include: skills, infrastructure, and various aspects of the business environment.[2] Access to affordable, reliable, and high-speed broadband infrastructure remains a problem in many parts of the world, including in parts of Europe, and in particular in rural and remote areas. It is important to foster continued efforts to provide high class affordable infrastructures, including as a locational determinant for businesses. It is also important to create a dynamic digital business environment and address concerns around digital entrepreneurship conditions in order to incentivise the creation of online services and applications. While this is also true for entrepreneurship more generally, it is even more important in the fast changing and fast moving digital world, and for digital entrepreneurs in startups, smaller companies, and newer companies, in highly innovative—and therefore inherently riskier—sectors.

Energising the business environment requires addressing issues related to the level of competition, entry and exit barriers, business creation, access to finance, bankruptcy regulation and legislation, data and privacy and security regulation, market fragmentation—especially for online and/or ICT-enabled services—and a perceived policy bias towards larger firms.[3] Inefficiency in all of these areas creates friction and costly regulatory uncertainty for (digital) entrepreneurs.

A Focus on Skills

Skills issues are tremendously important for digital entrepreneurship, from the ability to recruit talent, including across borders, to having the skills to identify new technology-enabled business opportunities and bringing them to fruition, either as a new venture, or by transforming existing ones.

Having the ability to communicate or "pitch" the business case for technology-enabled opportunities, either to the bank or other investors, or to senior management in the case of transforming activities in existing organisations, is crucial. This is an example of what is referred to as the need for "dual skills", or "e-leadership skills"[4] : people who combine an entrepreneurial mind-set and business skills and acumen with technical skills, at various levels of management and enterprise activity.

Business leaders need to possess a degree of technological awareness and understanding that allows them to identify new technologies that will transform and shape their business model; that will allow them to do new things, or do things differently, and to develop new products and services, ways of delivering them, and ways to communicate with their supplier, customers and employees. At the same time, technically trained people need business skills to identify new opportunities, but also the communication skills to convey them. Technical skills that are crucial in this environment include those of data scientists and engineers, specific big-data related skills and packages (such as Hadoop), data visualisation skills, service designers, user experience designers, and process engineering.[5]

As more countries transform into knowledge-based economies, and as the cloud and big data continue to gain importance, having access to these skills will become ever more important. Many countries are putting their hopes for economic development and innovation on investments in Information and Communication Technologies (ICTs). However, the impacts of ICTs depend on the use that is being made of them, which is in turn driven by factors such as skills, and whether or not the business environment enables people and businesses to take advantage of the opportunities offered by ICT. This is increasingly important in today's knowledge economies, in which "the creation, acquisition, dissemination, and utilisation of knowledge" are key to economic performance.[6]

In a fully enabled knowledge economy, different factors need to come together and mutually support each other to be able to maximise the opportunities for innovation, growth and competitiveness, and in particular: the physical ICT infrastructure, the soft infrastructure (the skills needed to exploit the physical infrastructure), the business environment (factors such as the cost and ease of starting a business, and product and labour market regulations), and the innovation environment (e.g., university and firm collaboration, ability to bring new ideas to market, treatment of R&D, IP protection).[7]

WHAT GOVERNMENTS CAN DO TO HELP

A good dose of regulatory humility will be needed in the fast moving digital space. Indeed, figuring out how to regulate activities and players that could be as yet unknown—created by fast moving and evolving technologies and the emergence of new applications—requires a fine balancing act.[8] Similarly, it will be important to find a balance between regulating for the protection of privacy and enhancing security on the user side, without restricting the opportunity for entrepreneurs to innovate and consumers to receive the benefits of this data-based innovation. Striving for consistency and harmonisation of the rules governing digital entrepreneurship, while also limiting regulatory change and uncertainty going forward, will also be critical. Several areas are key:

Ensuring the Supply of Appropriate Skills

Simplify and speed-up procedures for cross-border recruitment of talent and reduce costs (e.g. related to immigration rules and formalities); promote more interaction between the private sector and educational and training organisations to ensure the skills supply better matches the skills needs in practice.

Fostering a Competitive Environment

Reducing barriers to entry, and exit, where necessary is important in fostering a competitive environment and should help the diffusion of technology and reduce the power of incumbents.

Recognising the Self-Interest of Incumbents

Well-established businesses will often use policy influence to defend their market position against new disruptive technology based entrants. Policymakers need to be alert to these tactics and to ensure that policy intervention is not used as an unfair barrier to new competitive business models.

Clarifying the Rules for Use of Data

"Big data" regulation and rules of "ethical" conduct around the collection, storage and use of data are needed. But until the implications and ramifications of the big data era are better understood it will be important not to over-regulate, which could stifle innovation. At the same time, it is important to create trust in the online environment. Finding a balance between regulating for trust, and avoiding creating too much regulatory uncertainty and/or tie-downs will be an important and challenging task for policymakers.

Promoting Open Standards and Open Data

A new generation of evolved open standards will be required to unlock the full potential of the "internet-of-things". Policymakers should also "prime-the-pump" for the creation of new digital services by ensuring open access to public data (e.g. weather, traffic, geography, public records, archives) to allow the creation of new and relevant localised digital content, services and applications.

Recognising the "Sharing Economy"

Ensure rapid adaptation of regulatory regimes to enable "sharing economy" based business models and services this includes implementation of sensible IP protection and enforcement, adapted to the digital age.

Easing the Business Life Cycle

Simplify and harmonise regulation around starting and closing a business online—including bankruptcy laws—and around doing digital business, including across borders.

Creating the Best Climate for Incubation and Success

Promote entrepreneurship and technology awareness and skills in schools, at all levels, promoting technology skills, and especially combinations of technical and soft skills (e.g. communication, management, creative fields), and providing information and a one-stop-shop to start a business online.

Ensuring Access to Finance

Promote access to finance for startups and scale-ups, and strive for a culture where it is ok to try, fail and try again, which is very important as many successful—digital—enterprises have come about following many failed attempts.

Facilitating Market Integration and Demand Aggregation

Integrate markets for digital and online services by reducing fragmentation and other barriers, and help through the aggregation of demand where necessary to allow an increase in overall demand for ICT goods and services. And this includes enabling digital entrepreneurs to obtain cloud services from any provider, anywhere in the world and to be able to move data across borders.

CREATING THE CONDITIONS FOR DIGITAL GROWTH

Digital technologies offer tremendous growth opportunities but require entrepreneurs to have the ability to fully unlock their economic potential as the basis of new businesses or an enabler of the transformation of already established firms. Cloud computing dramatically reduces technical and investment barriers to bringing new digital products and services to market. But with these barriers being reduced much greater emphasis must be placed on creating the right conditions in the business environment—including skills, business cycle regulations, infrastructure and access to capital—that allow digital entrepreneurs to be successful. Access to the technology—even at scale—is no longer the limiting factor for digital entrepreneurial success and with that the role of policymakers in creating the right conditions for growth of new digital products and services becomes ever more critical.

Desirée van Welsum is senior ICT policy consultant, The World Bank and associate partner at Innovia Ventures

Jonathan Murray is co-founding partner of Innovia Ventures

NOTES

1. K. Kushida, J. Murray, and J. Zysman, "Diffusing the Cloud: Cloud Computing and Implications for Public Policy", *Journal of Industry, Competition and Trade,* 2011, http://ssrn.com/abstract=1861114 .
2. See T. Clayton and D. van Welsum, "Closing the Digital Entrepreneurship Gap in Europe: Enabling Businesses to Spur Growth", *The Conference Board*, Executive Action Report 425, 2014, The Conference Board, New York.
3. Ibid.
4. D. van Welsum and B. Lanvin, *e-Leadership Skills – Vision Report*, prepared for the European Commission, DG Enterprise and Industry, Octo-

ber 2012. Available for downloaded from the "e-Skills for Competitiveness and Innovation: Vision, Roadmap and Foresight Scenarios" project
website: http://eskills-vision.eu/results-downloads/ , or from the direct
link: http://eskills-vision.eu/fileadmin/eSkillsVision/documents/
Vision%20report.pdf .

5. See D. van Welsum, "The Digital Jobs of the Future", Chapter 1 of
The e-Skills Manifesto 2014, http://eskills-week.ec.europa.eu/c/document_
library/get_file?uuid=5bbbe47d-8d34-43d1-b602-f37d651047a8&
groupId=2293353 . Also available at: http://innoviaventures.com/the-
digital-jobs-of-the-future/ .

6. K. Kumar, and D. van Welsum, "Knowledge-Based Economies and
Basing Economies on Knowledge—Skills a Missing Link in GCC Coun-
tries," Research Report RR-188-GCC, The RAND Corporation, 2013,
Santa Monica, CA.

7. Similarly, see for example, the World Bank's Knowledge Assessment Methodology (KAM) framework which identifies four pillars to innovation processes (D. H. C. Chen and C. J. Dahlman, "The Knowledge
Economy, the KAM Methodology and World Bank Operations," Working
Paper, The World Bank, Washington D.C., October 19 2005): Economic
Incentive and Institutional Regime (policies and institutions for the protection of intellectual property, the rule of law, the ease of starting a business,
etc.), Education (human capital), Innovation (universities, firms and research institutes), and ICT (physical capital).

8. There is also a risk of regulatory "overshooting", for example in
response to the NSA and Snowden revelations, and some data security
breaches widely covered in the media. These have raised awareness and
brought much attention to the issue of data collection, use and storage,
privacy and security. In response, politicians, policymakers and regulators
feel the need to respond "firmly" to satisfy their stakeholders. This also
means that regulation in this area is currently (even more than usual) subject to change, creating additional uncertainty for companies. One example
of a likely "overreaction" were the calls for a "European NSA-proof internet" (European Internet services that are walled off from the US). As
recent as February 2014, Chancellor Merkel was still calling for such an
initiative and was inviting France for talks on the idea. However, it is
unlikely such "extreme" ideas could come to fruition, not least because it is
very likely they would not be successful in practice, for example because
of technical difficulties of implementing such a "solution", or with

American entities establishing themselves within Europe. There was also some talk of a "Schengen area for data". The idea was to create a "European cloud", and an area within which data traffic within Europe would be restricted to European channels. While this is unlikely to be successful because of how the internet is structured and operates, and also because traffic within such an area is only a fraction of all the online European activities, it would also create new burdens and costs for companies if they have to try to comply with such new restrictive rules.

III

A Roadmap for European Productivity Growth

TRANSFORM OR BE MARGINALISED: DOES EUROPE'S DIGITAL AWAKENING LIE AHEAD?

Nick Sohnemann

Google, Facebook and Twitter were not invented in Europe. The problem is that these companies *could not* have been invented in Europe either. They are the result of a unique digital innovation culture that is often referred to as Silicon Valley. The bad news for Europe is that this valley is driving the digitalisation process, and Europe is watching as a bystander.

The process of digitalisation is nothing new but has recently become faster and more powerful. In fact, the speed is breath-taking. Entire industries are being destroyed by digitalisation in ever shorter cycles. Video-rental businesses, for example, were destroyed by streaming platforms within no time at all. Before that it was the encyclopaedia business, which was destroyed by Microsoft Encarta and Wikipedia; the music industry, which was transformed by mp3, Apple's iTunes and Spotify; and the telecommunications sector, which was disrupted by Skype and WhatsApp.

Why are things so different now? For many years, experts have talked about digitalisation. But as a result of the continuous effect of Moore's law—which states that "the number of transistors and resistors (i.e., the computing power) on a chip doubles every 18 months"—the processing power has reached levels where every person with a laptop and Wi-Fi at home can change the world. The iPhone 6, for example, has twice the processing power of the iPhone 5 for the same price. So an entrepreneur nowadays can use a laptop and cloud computing to do everything from creating complex algorithms to establishing a global ecommerce platform

It is a new situation for Europe. Until now, digitalisation has represented a threat to many established industries. In some markets, digitalisation has taken away the middle man, such as real-estate agents and stock brokers. In other markets, such as publishing, advertising and music, it has diminished the profit margins. Some have created innovative marketplaces, like online auctions and e-commerce, or new forms of entertainment and communication such as video platforms and micro-blogging. Moreover, data-driven businesses have recently appeared, most notably Google and Facebook. Companies like this have never existed before. Nor has the consumer empowerment.

The problem is that 25 years after the advent of the internet, no European company is playing a major role in this digital development. The pressure is on. More and more industries have to transform to a digital core in the next five to 10 years—or they will be marginalised. Hence either Europe as a whole will transform and develop deep digital capabilities and understandings in all industries, or it will be pushed to the margins .

THE NEXT INDUSTRIES TO DIE

It has now become easier to anticipate the next industries to come under pressure. These include the banking and the energy sectors. In the banking sector, so-called "fintech" startups are taking business away from banks. Crowdfunding and peer-to-peer lending are replacing the traditional bank loans. Big data and predictive analytics are starting to replace so-called investment banking experts. In the energy sector, a push towards tracking and the democratisation of power supply are taking away the market dominance of the big suppliers—which still think in terms of coal and nuclear plants. In the new energy world, the consumers of energy will be producers too.

Here are a few more businesses that will be transformed:

- Self-driving cars will replace taxi drivers altogether. Moreover, for many it will be irrelevant to own a car, as mobility will be available everywhere.
- Drones will replace urgent delivery services. Thus, courier and postal services in this field will be replaced soon.
- Translation algorithms will destroy the markets for human translators.
- Robot journalists will challenge human writers on simple news tasks like sports and stock exchange news.

Human workforces will have to start reinventing themselves as computers continue to take on increasingly complicated tasks. The pattern is repeating itself: the incumbents are (European) big players—the disruptors are often startups or digital companies from the US. Of course, there are many European startups but they often do not have the same funding as American companies and not the same deep technological approach and support. In 2013 venture capital funds in the US invested $33bn in nearly 3500 investment rounds—in same year the venture capitalists in Europe invested merely a total of $7.4bn in approximately 1400 rounds.[1]

Technological advances have always been the driving force behind value and prosperity creation. But Europe has lost the edge in technological innovation. Recently, European companies have largely been concerned with globalisation. But globalisation is the opposite of technology. Globalisation is the process of bringing an established business to other countries—not about inventing a new business.

Globalisation was the driver in history that made Europe big in the past. But globalisation has a problem nowadays. It leads to more competition—since nearly all markets in the world are developed now—then to smaller margins and then to commoditisation. Technology is the core of something new. And new markets often mean big margins and a big impact.

THE IMPORTANCE OF INNOVATION CLUSTERS

Silicon Valley is the heart of digital innovations in the US, but while Silicon Valley may be the biggest tech hub in the US, it is not the only one—think Boston's Route 128; Austin, Texas; Seattle; Salt Lake City and so on. Europe does not have anything remotely similar to Silicon Valley. This valley is home to the leading digital companies in the world, including Google, Facebook and Airbnb, and has been created over a period of 40 years. Among the first companies that occupied the comparatively cheap land there were Intel and IBM. Stanford University—until then mostly a business university—suddenly started to offer programming and IT courses. More companies came to the region as the rent was cheap and the big city of San Francisco was not far away. Then, venture capitalists appeared and began funding new companies to take their place in this development.

Silicon Valley has now become more than a geographical region—it is an eco-system and a way of life. People who work and live there feel remarkably positive about the future and they want to solve problems. This ecosystem has grown organically over the years and hence is not easy to copy. It is a system that is reinforcing itself. Stanford is producing young engineering graduates who are looking for a job or looking to start a business. The big digital companies take them on board or venture capitalists give them funding to start their own business. It is what Stanford Professor Enrico Moretti calls a "brain hub" innovation cluster. It is similar to the hub for the car industry that Detroit was in the 1950s, but crucially Silicon Valley has been able to reinvent itself in recent history, from hardware, to software, to the web.

EUROPE'S SOLVABLE PROBLEMS

The advantage of a digital business is that there are hardly any marginal costs. The network effect is consequently a powerful driver for business success in the digital world. For example, the more people with accounts on Facebook, the more attractive it becomes for new users to sign up. A continent with many small nation states and language barriers will always have a disadvantage compared to the US given its large domestic market and homogenous language region. Every European startup and innovation therefore currently has a more difficult point to start from.

As an example, European startups are often simply underfunded. Funding for startups comes from domestic venture capitalists that focus on their small home markets. This leads to crazy situations. Mytaxi, a European taxi app, was sold for €50m to Daimler in 2014; whereas Uber, an American taxi app, received $1.2bn for 10 per cent of the company in 2014.

The established, big European digital companies are not a source for a European digital turnaround either. The two biggest, SAP and Vodafone, have been in existence for 42 years and 23 years respectively. Both are struggling with competition.

European businesspeople do not have a lot of experience with the possibilities of the digital world. In the past, European companies often viewed digital business as an add-on to their existing business, but not as a way to create something new. The crash of the first internet bubble between 2000 and 2001 was confirmation for the digital sceptics in Europe. The status quo was cemented. That is why there is a lack of experience with digital business today.

The network effect of digital business drives the emergence of monopolies, at least temporary ones until they are destroyed by the next digital transformer. Unfortunately, in Europe, economists, managers and policymakers still think in terms of entities of small and medium-sized companies, not in terms of world players. Silicon Valley is often driven by destroying markets and incumbents, and then recreating them. They call this the process of "creative destruction". Thus, the aim is to create world players not small and medium sized companies. Uber, for example, does not want to make the taxi market more efficient like Mytaxi, it wants to destroy the market and recreate it. It is foreseeable that Uber will become the world's dominant taxi app, while Mytaxi will be marginalised.

SEVEN GOLDEN RULES FOR EUROPE'S DIGITAL AWAKENING

So how can Europe get ready for the digital transformation? Here are the seven golden rules for Europe's digital awakening:

* *Establish one language in Europe.* We finally need one *lingua franca* in Europe in order to increase the power of the domestic market. This has to be English. It has to be mandatory for all Europeans to speak a proficient level of English.
* *The language of computer programming should become a third language in schools.* Once all schools teach the native language and English, the third language has got to be a programming language. This should be mandatory for all students. The motto should be "C++ instead of Spanish". This will help to enable digital thinking at a young age.
* *Enable European venture capital to become borderless.* The domestic market should always be Europe or the EU. This way, startups are not underfunded from the beginning and the market is always the entire EU. Policy barriers have to be lifted and investment cooperation should be encouraged—or even made mandatory for high-tech investment.
* *Change the data protection act.* The data protection laws in most countries are outdated. These should be updated and made relevant for the digital world where data is the new oil. In Germany, the last significant update to the data protection law happened in 1990—before the advent of the internet.
* *Stop the "fan culture" surrounding big, long-established companies.* Europe has too much respect for established businesses. The big European companies were largely created

after the Second World War. They should be subject to creative destruction, too. The universities prepare students to work at such companies. Instead, they should teach them to challenge those businesses and create new markets and innovations.

- *Europe needs more entrepreneurs.* Creating businesses has to be made simpler. We should learn from Portugal where it is now possible for entrepreneurs to start a new business online in less than one hour.
- *Stop copying the US—build our own digital DNA.* European digitalisation should not mean simply creating a European version of a US digital business. We need genuinely new value creation—not a European cloud or a European Silicon Valley, but our own new way of digital life. The aim should not be to attack Google with political measures, but European companies should try to tackle the worldwide digital market by attacking companies like Google through innovation, thereby creating better products. As Europe is already strong in high-quality manufacturing, transforming the process of production to digital could be the start of building our own digital DNA.

Nick Sohnemann is the founder and managing director of FutureCandy, an innovation consultancy, and head of the InnoLab at Hamburg Media School

NOTES

1. Dow Jones, "Dow Jones Venture Source", February 2014.

AN INNOVATION AGENDA FOR EUROPE

Paul Hofheinz

It has been more than a decade since Donald Rumsfeld, the hapless US secretary of defense, branded Europe's most advanced economies as "old Europe." The reaction at the time was merciless. German and French ministers decried the "polemics" as "unhelpful". But what if it were true? What if Europe's most advanced economies were truly "old" in some fundamental way? What if Europe was in fact stuck in genuine stasis, rendered immobile by interest group capture, complacency and ongoing strategic collapse?

Indeed, you could make such a case. But the good news about clichés is that, while they sometimes bear an element of truth, they often tell you more about the shallow judgements of the speaker than the true nature of the subject described. And they miss important changes taking place beneath the surface. The subterranean currents that, if encouraged to grow, could yet become mighty waves. Or the obscure call from the back of the room that eventually becomes a movement, and moves a nation.

REEVALUATING EUROPE

History walks along precisely these lines. It is a battle between the powerful tug of backward-looking obscurantism and the sometimes frightening imperative of embracing the modern and new. Both trends are there at the same time. Politics is where we strike the balance—the place where women and men seek to mitigate a middle ground between future and past.

Europe is no exception. Judging from the stories you read, you would think that the "old continent" is a lost cause. Seemingly unable to emerge from crisis, prone to discussions when action is needed, and hampered by a well-worn bag of economic policy tricks whose efficacy has long since passed its date of expiration. But what if the truth were more complex? What if the sometimes pointless debates in Europe were obscuring both real progress made and the potential for genuine leadership in areas where the modern will some day be truly defined? What if Europe actually had unheralded strengths in some areas that are ready to be developed and unleashed with the right set of policies?

What Europe needs is an economic policy based on embracing the modern and a generation of political leaders capable of making the case for it—and winning. There are promising signs that this generation may be slowly coalescing. Consider the following:

- In 2012, EU governments and businesses exported \$465bn of digitally deliverable services to the outside world, which was more than the US (\$383.7bn).[1]
- Four of the world's top five mobile app gaming companies are European—making this an area of genuine market-leading expertise.[2]
- Since 2011, the 18-member eurozone has run a monthly trade surplus, reaching an all-time high of €23bn in October 2014, up from the low of -€16bn in January 2011 at the crisis peak.[3] Most of the surplus comes from advanced manufactured goods, such as machinery and vehicles. Notably, France, Germany, Italy and the Netherlands—old Europe—make up the

lion's share of the surplus. Germany is the world's second largest exporter, selling a staggering €183bn of goods and services abroad in November 2014.[4]

FOUR KEY PRINCIPLES

So what does Europe need? What would it take to translate these islands of success into broader social and economic progress? An innovation agenda should be based on four principles: build, educate, open and learn.

Build

David Ricardo taught us long ago that trade is not based simply on one country selling things more cheaply than others. To the contrary, it is about each country finding its "competitive advantage"—the area where that country is able to produce the best goods at the most competitive price. For Europe, with its high wages and generous social welfare systems, this means high value-added products. Europe will not compete by making and selling low value-added goods.

High-end manufacturing is one area where Europe may have a competitive advantage. Germany points the way and shows what is possible. The country has focused relentlessly on delivering goods and services that define the cutting-edge of what is modern in advanced engineering. Even today, Germany is focusing on tomorrow, by developing a complex "Industrie 4.0" policy initiative, which is based on embracing the digital revolution in manufacturing. This involves retooling European production processes around advanced technology, including information and communication technology (ICT), and adding value into already well-made goods. It neatly embodies the best of both worlds: tying Germany's strength in manufacturing around the powerful tools of the future.

Educate

All modern economies need skilled workers. The European commission predicts that European companies will have more than one
million unfilled ICT vacancies across all industries in 2020. How
can this be possible when 24.4 million people—5.1 million of them
under the age of 25—are unable to find work?

Clearly, our education system is not providing the graduates we
need. If, as is true, more than 50 per cent of all jobs are created by
new companies, we need many more individuals who want to be,
and can be, entrepreneurs. Among the skills we need to teach are
basic entrepreneurial skills to give people the chance to create their
own opportunity and to employ others as they grow and scale up.
This is not a minor point. European industry will not return as the
jobs engine it was in *les trentes glorieuses*—the 30 years after the
Second World War—given our modern wage structure and the need
to become more productive.

Employment in Europe—when it does come—will arrive mostly
in new fast-growing companies formed around new products and
services, many of them based on the internet and digital technologies. We need to educate for these new realities, starting with digital
skills and entrepreneurship. People should not look only to large
companies as a source of future employment. They should be prepared—and educated—to be able to take the future into their own
hands, and perhaps even to give those large companies an innova-
tion-driven run for their money as well.

Open

Too many leading European companies—Prezi, Spotify and Storify
to name but three—move to Silicon Valley as soon as their products
show promise. But talk to these entrepreneurs and you hear an interesting story: it is not just about the easier access to capital they find
in California, though this is undoubtedly an advantage. It is the
huge, seamless market for digital goods and services in the US that

attracts them the most. 320 million consumers are linked by a common regulatory structure and a single language and market.

There is a lesson in this for Europe. If we want to help European entrepreneurs to create jobs, the best thing to do would be to open up the internal market, slashing through regulation that makes it hard to trade across borders (recent moves that dramatically complicate the cross-border VAT system are a case of movement in the wrong direction). Product standards in Europe must be high. But they should be standards that open markets, not standards that close or fragment them. Europe has the vision. But we must move to make this vision a reality by completing the digital single market and opening up a unified trading space where entrepreneurs can reach 507 million empowered consumers under one broadly-unified regulatory regime.

Learn

Although Europe has embraced the rhetoric of the "digital single market", the words are often spoken with a shallowness that belies their effect. On copyright, for example, Europe remains consumed with a useless tug of war between those who think the only reform copyright needs is tougher enforcement, and those who seek a more enabling environment where new businesses and business models can develop without threat of lawsuit or legal complications. We must develop a more open, pragmatic approach to policymaking in this key area, seeking to learn the lessons that market practice elsewhere teaches. The fair use doctrine in the US, for example, has made the US a vastly easier market for digital goods than Europe— and rights holders have hardly suffered. While fair use might not be the right policy for Europe, is there not scope for finding a similarly enabling mechanism within our copyright regime?[5]

Data is another area where politics triumphs over reason. Europe needs a workable data policy, where citizens receive the privacy protection they need and new data-driven businesses and services they deserve.[6] We must learn from evidence, and be prepared to move away from policy positions that have proven outdated or unproductive. The recent UK "non-paper" on the digital single market is a step in the right direction.[7]

INCLUSIVE GROWTH

Voters are sending policymakers a clear message. They are tired of stagnation and they want growth. The question is, as a society built on social inclusion—which aims to deliver full employment, educational opportunity and social justice—how do we move forward and deliver sustainable economic growth? The evidence tells us some interesting things. In advanced economies, innovation is by far the most important driver of prosperity and productivity, contributing between two-thirds and four-fifths of all economic growth.[8] Therefore, any economic growth strategy that ignores the all-important strand of promoting, encouraging and developing innovation is doomed to fail.

The nature of innovation is also changing. It is not just about a bunch of guys in white coats working in laboratories. It is also about the companies, services and new business models that entrepreneurs are building and leading—something that we have lots of here in Europe. We owe them a policy environment that works. And if we can deliver that, they will help us get where we need to be.

Paul Hofheinz is the executive director and co-founder of the Lisbon Council, a Brussels-based thinktank

NOTES

1. Joshua P. Meltzer, *The Importance of the Internet and Transatlantic Data Trade Flows for U.S. and EU Trade and Investment* (Washington, DC: Brookings, 2014).

2. Mark Mulligan and David Card, *Sizing the EU App Economy* (San Francisco: Gigaom, 2014).

3. Eurostat, *Euro Area International Trade in Goods Surplus €20.0 billion*, 15 January 2015, http://ec.europa.eu/eurostat/documents/2995521/6483786/6-15012015-AP-EN.pdf/a56f67b0-0767-46f5-ac02-686e409a5cab. In January 2015, Lithuania joined the euro, bringing the club to nineteen members.

4. Ibid.

5. The following report shows the way. The UK recently adopted legislation based on the report's conclusions. Ian Hargreaves, *Digital Opportunity: A Review of Intellectual Property and Growth*, 2011, https://www.gov.uk/government/uploads/system/uploads/attachment_data/file/32563/ipreview-finalreport.pdf.

6. Paul Hofheinz and Michael Mandel, *Bridging the Data Gap: How Digital Innovation Can Drive Growth and Create Jobs* (Brussels: The Lisbon Council, 2014).

7. See HM Government, *UK Vision for the EU's Digital Economy*, January 2015, http://www.engage.number10.gov.uk/digital-single-market/

8. Albert Bravo-Biosca, Louise Marston, Ann Mettler, Geoff Mulgan and Stian Westlake, *Plan I(nnovation) for Europe: Delivering Innovation-Led, Digitally-Powered Growth* (The Lisbon Council and Nesta, 2013).

GETTING EUROPE UP TO SCALE FOR THE ICT-ENABLED ECONOMY

Robert D. Atkinson

Achieving the goal of European progressives of opportunity for all will require a strong and growing economy. And the key to that is higher EU-wide productivity. After a long period during which Europe was closing the productivity gap with the US, since 1995 that gap has widened every year and shows no signs of narrowing. Indeed, if EU-15 productivity had grown at the same rate as US productivity from 1995 to 2013, EU-15 GDP would be €1.3tn greater than present levels. €1.3tn a year would mean higher real wages, lower government costs for social welfare expenditures and greater government revenues to support expenditures on needed public goods.

One key reason productivity has not grown as fast as in the US is that European nations have not been able to take as much advantage of the ICT revolution as has the US. This has been a particular problem not so much in creating European ICT firms to compete with the Facebooks and Googles of the world, but in all European firms in all kinds of industries being robust users of ICT technology. Around two-thirds of US productivity growth between 1995 and 2004 was due to ICT, and ICT has contributed roughly one-third of growth since then. Compared to the US, Europe has had far smaller productivity gains from ICT. And much of this lag has been in the services sector where productivity in European services industries grew only one-third as fast as it did in the US between 1995 and 2007.

ICTS BENEFIT FROM ECONOMIES OF SCALE

While there are a number of reasons for Europe's lag in using ICT one reason relates to scale. More than other technologies ICTs benefit from economies of scale. For example, it costs the same to develop a complex piece of logistics software for a trucking firm of 10,000 employees as 100 employees, but the former can amortise these costs over a much broader revenue base. This means the larger the market and the larger the organisation the easier it can be for an organisation to recoup its ICT investments.

However, Europe overemphasises the role of small firms in the economy in rhetoric and in policy. Indeed, for many progressives small firms have come to represent everything good in the economy with large firms representing all that is bad—they pollute, they offshore jobs, and so on. The reality, at least in the US, is that large firms are on average more productive, pay higher wages, injure and lay off their workers less, are more innovative, and export more. Larger firms are usually more productive, in part because they can take greater advantage of economies of scale when they invest in capital stock, including ICT. This is not to say that small firms do not add value. New firms that grow quickly, especially, create a significant share of net new jobs. But the large majority of small firms stay small, particularly in Europe where firm size is much more stable than in the US.

This does not mean that progressives need to be full-throated advocates for "big is beautiful". But it does mean that it is time to stop supporting policies tilted towards small firms, since the end result is lower productivity and income growth. Indeed, the European countries with the highest productivity tend to have far fewer small firms—Germany, Switzerland, and the UK have the smallest proportion of workers in small firms and have some of the highest labour productivity rates. On the other hand, Greece has very low productivity and has the highest percentage of small firms in Europe (two-thirds of Greek firms have under 20 workers).

Preferences for small businesses can take two forms: active policies to provide special benefits to small business; and discriminatory policies that place tax and regulatory burdens only on large businesses. The former policies, unless carefully targeted to potential high-growth "gazelle firms," simply keep the share of the economy produced by small businesses larger than it otherwise would be. The latter policies slow the growth of larger firms. For example, France's "anti-Amazon" law that prohibits discounts on books, including free shipping, raises prices for books from more efficient e-commerce channels, increasing the market share of smaller less productive book sellers. These kinds of rules, though, can also slow the growth of smaller firms that do not want to lose their special entitlements for being small if they get bigger than the threshold. France, for example, has a number of laws that apply only to businesses with 50 or more employees, and this provides an incentive for firms to stay under the 50-worker threshold.

A EUROPEAN SINGLE DIGITAL MARKET

It is not enough to level the playing field regarding firm size, Europe needs to level the playing field with regard to cross-national borders, and in particular create a European single digital market so that firms using ICT to provide goods or services can easily access customers in all 27 European nations. To be sure, Europe is moving in this direction. For example, it has taken some modest steps to rationalise the value-added tax for online sales. But it needs to go much further.

One key step is for Brussels to preempt national laws and regulations governing e-commerce in order to create one set of rules for firms trying to sell in Europe. Unfortunately, Europe has not done that. For example, Article 8 of Directive 99/44/EC on consumer sales states that member states can use more stringent provisions than the EC Directive. If the goal is only consumer protection, then setting an EU floor but allowing nations to adopt more stringent regulations can work. However, if the goal is a digital single market, Brussels needs to set a ceiling and floor that are the same: in other words, not let national governments set their own more stringent digital regulations.

Telecommunications is an area particularly ripe for a true digital single market. There are more than twice as many broadband providers in Europe than in the US and the small size of many European providers means higher costs and less capital to invest in world class networks. The European commission should work to enable much more consolidation and cross-border mergers of telecommunications companies. This is important in wireless as well, where the current fragmentation leads to high roaming charges (something the commission has attempted to solve by regulation) and slow roll out of 4G advanced networks. Brussels needs to create European-wide spectrum markets and allow firms to bid on spectrum auctions in all of Europe at once.

Streamlining VAT collection is another area in need of reform. E-commerce sellers are confronted with a complex mess of different tax rates, definitions and difficulties in calculating and remitting national VAT taxes. The solution is actually pretty straightforward: copy the US Streamlined Sales Tax Organisation effort where product definitions have been harmonised and free, easy-to-use plug-in software is available for e-commerce vendors that calculates, collects and remits VAT automatically. But individual European nations have little motivation to follow the US simplification path. To give them the incentive the European parliament should exempt e-commerce sales from national VATs unless the nation successfully participates and agrees to a "streamlined VAT process".

Europe also needs to ensure that its rules governing cloud computing enable a digital single market for this fast growing technology. Here the lesson is the opposite from VAT: there is no need for Brussels to step in and regulate cloud providers, especially providers of business services. EU businesses will still have legal responsibility based on national laws for data privacy and security even if they store data in the cloud in another EU nation (or non-EU nation). Firms cannot escape liability for data by giving it to a cloud provider, regardless of the location of the provider. This means that efforts to create "national clouds" or even European-only clouds, which some in Brussels have been promoting, would do nothing for commercial privacy or security, but, by balkanising the market, would lead to higher costs for cloud computing.

In addition, since most of the productivity gains from ICT are not from ICT industries but more traditional industries that adopt the use of ICT, it is important to encourage market integration in the latter industries as well. The 2014 European commission report on Single Market Integration finds that a number of countries, including Germany, France, Austria, and Belgium, stand in need of reforms to more fully open their service sectors with the rest of Europe. In particular, many professional services have national barriers to entry based on ensuring quality of service. While these barriers may serve important safety or quality goals, they may also function as barriers to competition and are not always worth their costs in public welfare.

Finally, it is not enough to create just a large integrated market in Europe, the goal should be to create an integrated transatlantic market through the Transatlantic Trade and Investment Partnership (TTIP). TTIP would significantly expand markets for many European firms by reducing non-tariff barriers in the US and increasing the ability of European companies to invest there. A recent report from Sweden estimates that European exports to the US could increase by 20 per cent to 40 per cent under the TTIP. These larger markets would increase the return on investment on more ICT projects for firms in the EU. And for progressives this should be a way to ensure that the two major regions of the world committed to the rule of law and democracy join together to show how globalisation is supposed to work.

Robert D. Atkinson is the founder and president of the Information Technology and Innovation Foundation (ITIF), a Washington, DC-based policy thinktank.

THE POLITICAL OPPORTUNITY OF THE DIGITAL AGE

Michael McTernan and Alastair Reed

The digitally-enabled economy is unleashing a new wave of change, something we are only just beginning to feel and understand. It increasingly appears that this will herald a "high opportunity, high risk society": whereby returns to entrepreneurship and skills will increase vastly and whole swathes of new jobs and industries will be created; but without concerted policy efforts this could occur alongside increased risks of being in low-paid or insecure employment, or having skills which quickly become surplus to requirements. This presents progressive politics with a renewed mission and purpose for the twenty-first century: to embrace ICT-based innovation as new ladders of inclusive growth, social mobility and job creation, while providing a new social investment-based welfare edifice for the digital age. [1]

The danger is that under the short-term pressures of the election cycle and at a time of widespread economic insecurity, progressives will shirk long-term decisions that will support and shape the environment for radical innovation and thus reinforce the low-growth, low-productivity cycle that consumes many European economies. If stuck defending the status quo, votes will continue to leak to new political competitors and populist insurgents. Electoral coalitions risk being further splintered by those who feel they benefit from technological change and those who do not.

ELECTORAL DILEMMAS OF DIGITALISATION

Many of Europe's progressive centre-left parties are under considerable strain as they struggle to absorb the aftershocks of the financial crisis and adapt to big structural changes related to globalisation and cultural and technological change. Their catch-all appeal—the ability to bridge the interests of voters from different socio-economic groups—has been severely dented by populists, new single issue parties, electoral abstention and broken political promises.

The contract that many parties made with their electorates over the past decade was premised on the assumption that globalisation would lift all boats and propel people into the new knowledge-based economy—delivering a more prosperous society for people's children. But today there is growing popular concern over inequality, which is increasingly affecting not just poorer and marginalised groups but many middle earners who are seeing their incomes stagnate. While for the first time in a generation, parents expect their children to grow up to be worse off than them.

One of the villains identified in driving these processes is technological change. This view is likely to increasingly take hold as the processes of digitisation continue to fuse with the winds of globalisation to affect not just lower skilled occupations but middle class occupations further-up the value chain. Research in the UK has shown that swathes of once sheltered and comfortable professions such as teaching, life sciences, engineers and accountants are showing a clear decline in their wage premiums over time as they are exposed to technological change and global competition.[2] Concerns over economic competitiveness and relative incomes may make these groups of voters more wary of taxation and redistribution—a key part of traditional centre-left political economy.[3] Meanwhile, "left-behind" working-class voters from the traditional heartlands of social democracy are becoming increasingly vulnerable to populist radical right parties as their prospects for employment and social mobility continue to recede, and as they perceive their values and priorities to be pushed to the margins of debate.[4]

If ill-managed, these tectonic shifts will have major consequences for longstanding electoral coalitions. It is not hard to foresee a scenario whereby mainstream parties are flanked by insurgent parties offering quick fixes to issues arising from technological change—pulling them from the centre ground. Just as populists made significant gains in recent years by playing on fears arising from globalisation, new techno-populists will emerge playing off fears arising from digitalisation. There are also likely to be heightened tensions and distributional conflicts between labour market "outsiders" and "insiders"—those with stable jobs and those in more precarious employment or without a job. Tech-savvy young people may gain a foothold at the expense of older workers; while women may benefit more from the flexible nature of the internet-enabled "sharing economy", resulting in their political preferences changing as we move decisively from the male bread-winner model and traditional working patterns.

Voters may, of course, hanker for quick fixes if that is all that is offered to them. But equally, as voters' livelihoods become increasingly risky they may value new institutions that provide them with greater security and the means to succeed. The big policy responses to the industrial revolution—welfare states, public health services, and education—developed into institutions with widespread public support, albeit challenged somewhat in recent times. Similarly, new institutions that reflect the new political realities—not least a more individualistic society and one less trusting in the state to spend taxpayers' money—can flourish. This also chimes with the enabling role that new technology can offer, with vast potential for social mobility: the internet has led to an array of affordable and creative platforms for learning, communicating, trading, entrepreneurialism and collaborating.[5]

SAILING WITH THE WINDS OF CHANGE

Confronted with these challenges, however, there is a temptation for progressives to ignore the horizon and focus on preserving the achievements, institutions and "way of life" of the twentieth century. The historian Tony Judt articulated this in his final book *Ill Fares the Land,* arriving at the position of a defensive social democracy that sides with those threatened with economic extinction and focuses on preservation and prudence in an age of fear.[6] These sentiments, as Rob Atkinson has set out in the introduction to this volume, are leading some to take uncompromising positions on global integration and trade (examples include positions on the Digital Single Market and the proposed EU–US Transatlantic Atlantic Trade and Investment Partnership), and protecting incumbent industries or firms at the expense of more nimble and productive competitors.[7] There is, in short, a hesitance to embrace the Schumpeterian growth imperative that pervades this volume—and to support productivity and innovation-enhancing growth policies through the more ubiquitous adoption of ICT by all organisations (for profit, non-profit and government) through-out the economy. But such a strategy, while certainly fostering some disruption in the short-term, will make the progressive project easier in the medium and long-term by boosting growth, which will support both higher incomes and increased state revenues.

At a time of low job growth and anaemic productivity it is important to seize and shape this agenda. The US has been far more successful than Europe in adopting ICT across the economy, thereby driving productivity. If the US and EU-15 had swapped productivity growth rates from 1995 to 2013, it is estimated that EU-15 GDP would be €2.2tn larger than the US, instead of €1.6tn smaller.[8]

That said, it is important not to present this debate in the black and white terms of "techno-optimism" trumping backward-looking "techno-pessimism". There are many reasons to be cautious: without the requisite socio-economic policies, the disruption and job-destroying side of automation and technological change could considerably hamper political stability, government and business. Job insecurity will be a growing concern as the world of work is fundamentally altered. The future labour market is likely to be highly competitive, and employees are going to have to upskill for a world of fewer long-term contracts. Trades unions have a vital role to play here. And we are entering an unknown and unprecedented world of technology interacting with the environment and human nature, chiefly in the form of biotech, nanotech and Artificial Intelligence.[9]

A PROGRESSIVE APPROACH TO RADICAL INNOVATION

So how should progressives respond? First, all of the above opportunities and risks underline the need for progressive politics and a rethinking of the role of the state. There is a new purpose in navigating and supporting capitalist models through their next phase of creative destruction and in leveraging technology to tackle the great societal challenges of our times. This should not signal a politics of obstruction based upon futile attempts by national governments to impede the technological advancement that is transforming the global economy. Technology may radically alter how the world functions, but socio-political choices matter. The terrain of social democracy in the twenty-first century should be to enable and guide the unleashing of these forces, while ensuring that everyone can share in the benefits of these new opportunities.

Second, progressives need to embrace the potential of innovation and technological change. Promoting innovation by investing in science and R&D is the easy part politically—given that this is a largely uncontroversial intervention for those on the left or right—but dealing with the impact of innovation on specific industries and local communities is more challenging. The short-term "losers" from change are typically easier to identify and louder, but the benefits can be spread across society and over time. This is particularly evident in public services. Technology can help achieve unprecedented improvements in productivity and outcomes—such as by introducing massive open online courses, or MOOCS, to broaden access to elite higher education—but this will impact the jobs and practices of public sector workers, a key part the centre-left's traditional power base. Politicians need to be straight with voters that these headwinds will have both positive and negative consequences, and be careful not to champion incumbents and rent-seekers in the name of social justice. Progressives can also champion technology policies that seek to reduce the number of low-wage, unsafe and unsatisfying jobs—automating many of these jobs, while at the same time coupling this with strong efforts to boost people's skills.

Crucially, promoting innovation is also about new forms of de-centralised institutions, as the micro and regional-levels are more suited to the age and spirit of the time. Despite the world becoming more connected, the importance of place has increased. As Silicon Valley in the US highlights, the nature of the innovative process means that people and companies are keen to cluster together to benefit from so-called "network effects", putting different localities on increasingly divergent paths.

Third, a radically new concept of social investment is required which renews welfare edifices for the twenty-first century. Gone are the days of a job, or even a career, for life. Government, trades unions and businesses need to collaborate on new forms of protection, investment and flexibility, as well as on lifelong learning. New forms of social investment in education and skills are required to enable people from all backgrounds to harness the potential of technology and meet the demands of rapidly changing labour markets, whether they work for themselves or for someone else.

Fourth, progressives need to work together to forge a European innovation agenda and deliver an EU digital single market. They also need to make the case for international cooperation and openness more than ever, given the international footprints of modern, technology-enabled businesses. New institutions, regulatory approaches and tax systems are required which are fit for the digital age, but these must be agreed internationally if they are to be effective. And this needs to include a commitment by progressives across nations to support efforts to fight anti-competitive "innovation mercantilism" in nations like China and Brazil.

Innovation is about the constant transformation of an economy and its institutions. By its nature some industries and firms will lose out as new challengers take advantage of productivity and environmental improvements and create new jobs and value. Rather than trying to stop this perennial gale, managing the transition into new work and creating new forms of social investment should be the key mission of progressive politicians in the twenty-first century. In political terms, there is a significant first mover advantage to be had for the parties and governments that cater to, adapt to and shape the new digital economy.

Michael McTernan is acting director of Policy Network, a London-based international thinktank and network.

Alastair Reed is a researcher at Policy Network.

NOTES

1. The term "high risk, high opportunity society" was used by Antony Giddens in a lecture at the London School of Economics. See *Off the Edge of History: The World in the 21st Century*, London School of Economics, 19 February 2013.

2. Stephen Machin and Brian Bell, "Clinging on to Middle Class Life?", Policy Network, 15 April 2014, http://www.policy-network.net/pno_detail.aspx?ID=4622&title=Clinging-on-to-a-middle-class-life. See also Carl Benedict Frey and Michael Osbourne, "One-Third of Jobs in the UK at Risk from Automation", Deloitte study, 10 November 2014, http://www2.deloitte.com/uk/en/pages/press-releases/articles/deloitte-one-third-of-jobs-in-the-uk-at-risk-from-automation.html.

3. Anne Wren, *The Political Economy of the Service Transition* (Oxford: Oxford University Press, 2013).

4. See Matthew Goodwin and Rob Ford, *Revolt on the Right: Explaining Support for the Radical Right in Britain* (London: Routledge, 2013).

5. See Matthew Taylor, "The Power to Create", *RSA Blog*, http://www.matthewtaylorsblog.com/thersa/the-power-to-create-in-about-5-minutes/

6. Tony Judt, *Ill Fares the Land* (London: Allen Lane, 2010).

7. Robert D. Atkinson, "The Progressive Power of Creative Destruction" (The introduction to this publication).

8. Ben Miller and Robert D. Atkinson, "Raising European Productivity Growth Through ICT", Information Technology and Innovation Foundation, June 2014.

9. Ibid.